D0778564

NAMES
OF THE
DEAD

Also by Diane Schoemperlen

Red Plaid Shirt

Our Lady of the Lost and Found

Forms of Devotion

In the Language of Love

Hockey Night in Canada and Other Stories

The Man of My Dreams

Hockey Night in Canada

Frogs and Other Stories

Double Exposures

NAMES OF THE DEAD

An Elegy for the Victims of September 11

Diane Schoemperlen

VIKING

VIKING
Published by the Penguin Group
Penguin Group (USA) Inc., 375 Hudson Street, New York, New York 10014, U.S.A.
Penguin Books Ltd, 80 Strand, London WC2R 0RL, England
Penguin Books Australia Ltd, 250 Camberwell Road, Camberwell, Victoria 3124, Australia
Penguin Books Canada Ltd, 10 Alcorn Avenue, Toronto, Ontario, Canada M4V 3B2
Penguin Books India (P) Ltd, 11 Community Centre, Panchsheel Park, New Delhi—110 017, India
Penguin Group (NZ), Cnr Airborne and Rosedale Roads, Albany, Auckland 1310, New Zealand
Penguin Books (South Africa) (Pty) Ltd, 24 Sturdee Avenue, Rosebank, Johannesburg 2196, South Africa

Penguin Books Ltd, Registered Offices: 80 Strand, London WC2R 0RL, England

First published in 2004 by Viking Penguin, a member of Penguin Group (USA) Inc.

10 9 8 7 6 5 4 3 2 1

Page 237 constitutes an extension of this copyright page.

LIBRARY OF CONGRESS CATALOGING IN PUBLICATION DATA
Schoemperlen, Diane.
Names of the dead: an elegy for the victims of September 11 / Diane Schoemperlen
p. cm.
ISBN 0-670-03325-1
1. September 11 Terrorist Attacks, 2001. 2. Victims of terrorism.
3. Terrorism. I. Title
PR911.3.S267N36 2004
811'.54—dc22 2003066565

This book is printed on acid-free paper. ♾

Printed in the United States of America
Set in Perpetua
Designed by Francesca Belanger

NAMES OF THE DEAD

An Elegy for the Victims of September 11

Diane Schoemperlen

VIKING

VIKING
Published by the Penguin Group
Penguin Group (USA) Inc., 375 Hudson Street, New York, New York 10014, U.S.A.
Penguin Books Ltd, 80 Strand, London WC2R 0RL, England
Penguin Books Australia Ltd, 250 Camberwell Road, Camberwell, Victoria 3124, Australia
Penguin Books Canada Ltd, 10 Alcorn Avenue, Toronto, Ontario, Canada M4V 3B2
Penguin Books India (P) Ltd, 11 Community Centre, Panchsheel Park, New Delhi—110 017, India
Penguin Group (NZ), Cnr Airborne and Rosedale Roads, Albany, Auckland 1310, New Zealand
Penguin Books (South Africa) (Pty) Ltd, 24 Sturdee Avenue, Rosebank, Johannesburg 2196, South Africa

Penguin Books Ltd, Registered Offices: 80 Strand, London WC2R 0RL, England

First published in 2004 by Viking Penguin, a member of Penguin Group (USA) Inc.

10 9 8 7 6 5 4 3 2 1

Page 237 constitutes an extension of this copyright page.

LIBRARY OF CONGRESS CATALOGING IN PUBLICATION DATA
Schoemperlen, Diane.
Names of the dead: an elegy for the victims of September 11 / Diane Schoemperlen
p. cm.
ISBN 0-670-03325-1
1. September 11 Terrorist Attacks, 2001. 2. Victims of terrorism.
3. Terrorism. I. Title
PR911.3.S267N36 2004
811'.54—dc22 2003066565

This book is printed on acid-free paper. ♾

Printed in the United States of America
Set in Perpetua
Designed by Francesca Belanger

He healeth the broken in heart,
and bindeth up their wounds.
He telleth the number of the stars;
he calleth them all by their names.

—Psalm 147:3–4

Alphabet of names in a green field.
Names in the small tracks of birds.
Names lifted from a hat
Or balanced on the tip of the tongue.
Names wheeled into the dim warehouse of memory.
So many names, there is barely room on the walls of the heart.

—Billy Collins, "The Names"

Why love what you will lose?
There is nothing else to love.

—Louise Glück, "From the Japanese,"
in *The Triumph of Achilles*

[G]rief is the stringing together of facts, like the beads of a necklace.

—*New York Times,* Portraits of Grief Series,
"Elvin Romero: A Daughter's Questions," November 24, 2001

[E]ven if every scrap of a life were saved, thrown into a giant
mound and then carefully sifted to extract all possible meaning,
it would not add up to a life.

—Siri Hustvedt, *What I Loved*

Preface

This book is a work of both extensive research and the imagination. It is at once a distillation and an elaboration of the facts.

I began with the names. At that time, it was only two months since the tragedy and the lists of victims were incomplete and incorrect. I worked solely from the Internet, using the lists posted by the Associated Press, the *New York Times,* the *Washington Post,* and CNN. All the lists were different. All the lists changed every day: names added, names deleted, spellings changed and then changed back again. Nobody knew yet how many people had died.

For four months I worked only on the names.

Listing the names of the dead on memorials to tragedies involving large-scale loss has become an established practice all over the world. The names of the dead appear on monuments commemorating lives lost in both World Wars and in the 1995 Oklahoma City bombing, in Israel's memorial to the Holocaust, Yad Vashem, and on Maya Lin's Vietnam Memorial wall in Washington, D.C. In all such lists there is an immediate recognition of the power of naming, this deceptively simple way in which we bestow identity and individuality upon others and ourselves. Reading a long list of the names of the dead becomes almost overwhelming as it goes on and on, so simply and brutally conveying the magnitude of all that was lost. Faced with such large losses of life, we find that the *numbers* of the dead tend to remain as abstractions in the mind but the *names* . . . the names are real. They take your breath away with their power. They can only be read with your heart in your mouth.

Finally, arranged in paragraphs, the names of the September 11 victims totaled more than eighty pages in manuscript.

While working on the names, I was also reading profiles and obituaries of the victims, personal accounts by survivors, as well as many factual and photographic books about the tragedy. I began to figure out what I wanted to put into all those blank spaces between the paragraphs of names.

I immersed myself in elegaic poetry in an attempt to discover the right tone, the delicate balance between lyricism and cold hard fact, between joy and despair. I read the work of many individual poets, and I studied an anthology called *Inventions of Farewell: A Book of Elegies,* edited by Sandra M. Gilbert and published by W. W. Norton and Company. It contains more than two hundred poems by writers from Shakespeare, Donne, Wordsworth, Dickinson, and Yeats to Walt Whitman, Dylan Thomas, Gerard Manley Hopkins, and Tennyson to Sharon Olds, Alice Walker, Rita Dove, Philip Larkin, and Sylvia Plath. I read Rilke's *Duino Elegies* several times. From each of the poems I read, I learned something more about how to write about death, how to speak beautifully about the unspeakable. I carried Elie Wiesel's memoir of the Holocaust, *Night,* in my purse for weeks.

Of utmost importance for inspiration, reassurance, structure, and style in this book was a collection of essays by Susan Griffin called *A Chorus of Stones: The Private Life of War,* published by Doubleday in 1992. The last essay in the book, "Notes Toward a Sketch for a Work in Progress," is about the paintings and writings of Charlotte Salomon, which were published in a book called *Life? Or Theatre?: A Play with Music.* The nearly eight hundred paintings in this book tell the story of Salomon's short life. She was born into a wealthy Jewish family in Berlin in 1917. In 1943, pregnant, she was sent to her death at Auschwitz. Griffin uses a fragmentary collagelike structure to write about Salomon, including her thoughts on writing about Salomon, on her own life, and on the Gulf War, which begins while she is writing the essay. Many passages in this hundred-page essay described exactly what I was trying to do in *Names of the Dead* as well as the problems I was encountering.

Griffin writes: "There are so many stories I heard in the course of the writing that I would like to include in the book. But one cannot tell everything. The urgency of testimony, of bearing witness. A crowd pressing, like passengers, pushing to board a train already filled to capacity. . . . Even in the retelling of one story, so many details have had to be left out. And others are given a new prominence. That is, I give them a prominence. And then the book itself, moving with its own life, makes certain choices which I must obey."

I knew from the beginning that I didn't want to write descriptions of the burning towers or details of the horrors that went on inside the buildings or the hijacked planes. Nor did I want to write about the politics of the event or my own reaction to the tragedy. In the face of it, my personal reaction was certainly no more important than anyone else's. I wanted to write a book in which I did not appear. I knew that somehow all the victims had to be included in the book. To me, each person was of equal importance. They were all so different and yet there were so many similarities, too. How could I possibly give each of them a voice? I knew that I wanted to write primarily about the *lives* of the victims. We all knew about their deaths. I wanted to capture moments of their lives up to that moment.

Many of the fragments I have included are obviously factual in nature: for instance, the chronology of the day's events, the technical information on the Boeing 767 and 757, the structural information on the World Trade Center and the Pentagon, the business information on Windows of the World and Cantor Fitzgerald, and the lists of collapsed and damaged buildings. Each detail included immediately after a victim's name is also completely factual, including relationships between victims, birthdays, anniversaries, upcoming weddings and births, ages of surviving children, and so on.

The fragments that appear in series are also solely products of my research, drawing together and distilling the details of many individuals' lives as described in their profiles and obituaries. These include the following series: "Tuesday morning," "Distinguishing features" (including tattoos), "Last seen wearing" (both clothing and jewelry), "The future," "The past," "The things they carried," "The things they loved," "The things they hated," "Former lives," "Military honors," "Occupations," "Favorite books" (also favorite foods, movies, and television shows), "Police," "Secrets," and "What remains."

In reading about the victims, I found that many things were mentioned over and over again: taking the children to the park, buying a new house, going grocery shopping, renovating, and so on. I decided I had to find a way to write about these common activities without mentioning any one person by name, thereby telling the story of an individual while at the same time using that small story to represent the stories of many others. Therefore, each narrative fragment appearing in a separate paragraph does tell a specific story, but it is not intended to refer directly to the name that immediately precedes it.

Beginning with the facts found in the profiles of the victims, I then elaborated from that to create short narrative scenes of events that had happened in the lives of the victims. Virtually all of the fragments of a narrative nature began with something I discovered in my research. For instance, in one profile it was noted that the individual was especially fond of the book *A Short Guide to a Happy Life,* by Anna Quindlen, and had given copies of it to all his friends. I felt free to imagine this in further detail and to include a passage from that book that he might have liked the most. The series called "On the desk" and "In the dream" were also written in this way. Many profiles mentioned what the individuals had kept on their desks. I then imagined these family pictures, trophies, cards, and other mementos in detail. The dreams included here were all also described in the profiles.

Only a very few fragments are wholly the product of my imagination. These include the short descriptions of ordinary objects and events, such as a bowl of fruit on the kitchen table, candles and Legos on the coffee table, seeing a dead rat on the sidewalk, hearing the sounds of trains and rain and thunder in the night. Also imagined are the things the victims might have been planning to do on that Tuesday afternoon, such as clean out their desks, ask for a raise, or answer all their e-mails.

The fragments describing what they did that Monday evening are factual, except for the ones that have them making love: these are my invention.

I did not know anyone who died on September 11. But for weeks at a time I felt closer to these three thousand dead people that I had never met than I did to anyone in my own life. As François Mauriac wrote in his foreword to *Night:* "It is not always the events we have been directly involved in that affect us the most."

NAMES
OF THE
DEAD

A

Gordon McCannel Aamoth Jr. Edelmiro (Ed) Abad. Maria Rose Abad.

Tuesday, third day of the week, named for Tiu, the Germanic god of war and the sky.

Andrew Anthony Abate. Vincent P. Abate. Brothers. Best friends of **Michael A. Uliano,** also killed.

Laurence Christopher Abel. Alona Abraham. William F. Abrahamson. Richard Anthony Aceto. Heinrich Bernhard Ackermann.

September. A month of returning and beginning: back to work, back to school, back to the regular routine; a new season, a new job, a new project; a month that for many marks the beginning of a new year more than New Year's itself. A month of sharpened pencils, new shoes, the look of the leaves just before they start to turn. A month of optimism and renewed energy after the humid languor of summer. A change in the air, a change in the light, a change in the color of the sky. It was a beautiful morning. It was the eleventh day of the ninth month: 911.

Paul Andrew Acquaviva. Expectant father. His second child, a boy, was born on December 20, 2001.

Christian Adams. Donald LaRoy Adams. Patrick Adams. Shannon Lewis Adams. Stephen George Adams.

Begin with a prayer.
A prayer for courage, comfort, mercy, strength.

Ignatius Udo Adanga. Christy A. Addamo. Terence E. Adderley Jr. Sophia Buruwad Addo. Lee Allan Adler.

Begin with a promise.
A promise to bear witness, to honor, never to forget.

Daniel Thomas Afflitto Jr. Expectant father. On September 11, his first child, a boy, was six months old. On September 12, his wife found out she was pregnant with their second child. The baby, a boy, was born on May 20, 2002.

Emmanuel Akwasi Afuakwah. Alok Agarwal. Mukul Kumar Agarwala. Joseph Agnello, firefighter, Ladder Company 118; posthumously promoted to lieutenant. **David Scott Agnes. João Alberto DaFonseca Aguiar Jr.**

At 7:59 a.m. Eastern Daylight Time, American Airlines Flight 11, a Boeing 767, leaves Logan Airport in Boston, Massachusetts, bound for Los Angeles, California, with eighty-one passengers and eleven crew members aboard.

Lieutenant Brian G. Ahearn, firefighter, Engine Company 230. **Jeremiah Joseph Ahern. Joanne Marie Ahladiotis. Shabbir Ahmed. Terrance André Aiken. Godwin Ajala.**

Father. Mother. Sister. Brother. Son. Daughter. Grandmother. Grandfather. Grandson. Granddaughter. Aunt. Uncle. Niece. Nephew. Cousin.

Gertrude M. (Trudi) Alagero. September 7 was her thirty-seventh birthday.

Andrew Alameno.

Husband. Wife. Boyfriend. Girlfriend. Best friend. Fiancé. Fiancée. Lover. Partner. Companion. Roommate. Brother-in-law. Sister-in-law. Neighbor. Unborn child.

Margaret Ann (Peggy) Jezycki Alario. September 18 was her forty-second birthday.

Gary M. Albero. Jon Leslie Albert. Peter Craig Alderman. Jacquelyn Delaine Aldridge-Frederick. Grace Yu Alegre-Cua. David Dewey Alger. Ernest Alikakos. Edward L. Allegretto.

Christian. Jew. Muslim. Hindu. Buddhist. Atheist. Undecided.

Eric Allen, firefighter, Squad 18. **Joseph Ryan Allen. Richard Dennis Allen,** firefighter, Ladder 15.

September 10. A cloud of ambient anxiety had shadowed her for days. She kept trying to push it away but always it returned: an oppressive weight growing by increments every hour, a burden of disquiet percolating all through her body. No matter what she was doing—filing papers at work, riding the subway home, helping her son with his homework, braiding her daughter's hair—she felt heavy and uneasy. On Monday night she couldn't sleep. Her heart was racing. She found it hard to breathe and there was a pain in her chest. She got out of bed and turned on all the lights. Her children sighed in their sleep. She sat in the kitchen and looked out at the night. The pain went away but the anxiety did not. She knew something terrible was going to happen but she didn't know what or when or to whom. On Tuesday morning she got up and went to work.

Richard Lanard Allen. Best friend of **Sean Booker,** also killed.

Christopher Edward Allingham. Anna S. Williams Allison. Janet M. Bohlander Alonso. Anthony Joshua Alvarado. Antonio Javier Alvarez. Victoria (Sandra) Alvarez-Brito. Telmo E. Alvear.

September 10. In bed that night the husband heaved a deep sigh of contentment and said, All our dreams are finally coming true. The wife agreed. They had never been happier. On Monday night they fell asleep quickly and slept soundly. On Tuesday morning they got up and went to work.

César Amoranto Alviar. He had been married three times to the same woman: first in a civil ceremony, then in a church ceremony, and finally, three years ago, they had renewed their wedding vows after twenty-five years of marriage.

Tariq Amanullah. Angelo Amaranto. Captain James M. Amato, firefighter, Squad 1; posthumously promoted to battalion chief. **Joseph Amatuccio.**

Tuesday morning. She was scheduled to fly home several days earlier but decided to stay longer; her husband took the original flight as planned. She was supposed to fly on Monday but her flight was delayed by a thunderstorm so she decided to fly on Tuesday morning instead. They were scheduled to take a later flight on Tuesday, but they got to the airport early and changed their tickets. She had changed her trip home four times before ending up on a Tuesday-morning flight.

Paul Wesley Ambrose. He became engaged at the beginning of September.

Christopher Charles Amoroso, police officer, Port Authority of New York and New Jersey. **Specialist Craig S. Amundson. Kazuhiro Anai. Calixto (Charlie) Anaya Jr.,** firefighter, Engine 4.

Tuesday morning. He was originally scheduled to fly on Monday but was called for one day of jury duty and changed his trip to Tuesday instead. She was supposed to be on a later flight but changed to an earlier one that was less crowded. He was originally scheduled to fly on Monday but his flight was canceled due to a fire at Newark Airport, so he decided to fly on Tuesday morning instead. She was supposed to be on a different flight but changed to one that was nonstop. He was supposed to fly on Monday, but a reservation error had him traveling on Tuesday instead.

Joseph Peter Anchundia. Best friend and roommate of **Judson J. Cavalier,** also killed.

Kermit Charles Anderson. Yvette Constance Anderson. John (Jack) Andreacchio. Michael Rourke Andrews. Jean Ann Andrucki. Siew-Nya Ang.

Driving to the airport. Although it was early, the traffic was already starting to build, the sun glinting off the cars all around them. The husband put on his sunglasses and sighed. It was just another business trip: he would be home on Thursday night. Usually he enjoyed these little jaunts, but this time he was tired. He really didn't want to go; maybe he was coming down with something, maybe he just needed a break. Maybe next week he would take a couple of days off. His wife, who was driving, said that sounded like a good idea. They pulled up in front of the terminal. They kissed and his wife said, Will you call me when you get there? He said, Of course I will. Don't I always? He reminded her of their daughter's dentist appointment the next morning. They kissed again, and he got his small suitcase out of the trunk and walked into the terminal.

Joseph J. Angelini Sr., firefighter, Rescue Company 1. **Joseph J. Angelini Jr.,** firefighter, Ladder 4. Father and son. Joseph Sr. was the most veteran firefighter in New York City, with forty years on the job.

David Lawrence Angell. Lynn Edwards Angell. Husband and wife.

Laura Angilletta. Doreen J. Angrisani.

Absence.

Lorraine Del Carmen Antigua. September 27 was her thirty-third birthday.

Seima Aoyama.

Accountant. Actor. Administrator. Advertising manager. Air-conditioning technician. Analyst. Antenna engineer. Antiques dealer. Arborist. Architect. Assistant chef. Assistant wine master. Astronautical engineer. Attorney. Audiovisual technician. Auditor. Aviation warfare systems operator.

Peter Paul Apollo. September 23 was his twenty-seventh birthday. He was to be married on November 16, 2001.

Faustino Apostol Jr., firefighter, Battalion 2. **Frank Thomas Aquilino. Patrick Michael Aranyos.**

At 8:14 a.m. United Airlines Flight 175, a Boeing 767, leaves Logan Airport in Boston, Massachusetts, bound for Los Angeles, California, with fifty-six passengers and nine crew members aboard.

David Gregory Arce, firefighter, Engine 33. Lifelong best friend of **Michael Boyle,** firefighter, Engine 33, also killed. Their bodies were found together and subsequently buried side by side.

Michael George Arczynski. Expectant father. His seventh child, a girl, was born on February 16, 2002.

Louis Arena, firefighter, Ladder 5. **Barbara Jean (Bobbi) Arestegui,** flight attendant, American Airlines Flight 11.

Apocalypse.

Adam P. Arias. September 5 was his third wedding anniversary. During their marriage, his wife had undergone fifteen lymphoma-related surgeries. In October 2001 she had her sixteenth operation.

Michael Joseph Armstrong. He was to be married on October 6, 2001.

Jack Charles Aron. Joshua Todd Aron. Richard Avery Aronow. Myra Joy Aronson. Yaphet Jesse Aryee. Carl Francis Asaro, firefighter, Battalion 9.

Tuesday morning. September 11 was his first day of work at a new job. September 11 was her first day back at work after a week's vacation. September 11 was the only day that week that he was scheduled to be in the office. September 11 was his second day of work at a new job. September 11 was his last day of work before a two-week vacation. September 11 was his last day of work before beginning a new job elsewhere. September 11 was his last day of work before his wedding on the weekend; his fiancée worked for the same company but she stayed home on Tuesday to complete the wedding preparations.

Michael A. Asciak. Michael Edward Asher. Janice Marie Ashley. Thomas J. Ashton. Manuel O. Asitimbay. Lieutenant Gregg Arthur Atlas, firefighter, Engine 10.

Distinguishing features. Small chicken-pox scar above his left eyebrow. Hairline scar below her stomach. Burn scars on his right foot. Left arm and leg two inches shorter than the right, small mole above his upper lip. Two-inch raised red appendectomy scar. Gallbladder scar on his stomach, scar on his left palm near the thumb. Dark circles under her eyes. Deep stretch marks under his arms. Quadriplegic. Scars from bunion operations on both feet. Green birthmark on his lower back. Freckles. Permanent braces on her inside bottom teeth. Small hole in cartilage at top of his right ear. Strawberry-shaped birthmark above her belly button. Tip of his left middle finger missing. Horizontal cesarean scar on bikini line, one-inch scar on the sole of her foot (not sure which foot).

Gerald T. Atwood, firefighter, Ladder 21. Expectant father. His third child, a boy, was born on March 2, 2002.

James Audiffred. Louis Frank Aversano Jr. Ezra Aviles.

Last seen wearing. Gray pinstripe suit, white shirt, dark tie. Black pinstripe Gucci suit with tapered pants, white cotton blouse with spread collar. Green-striped button-down shirt, gray slacks, black shoes. Black jacket and skirt, white sneakers. Powder-blue pantsuit. Black cashmere sweater and black slacks. Long-sleeved Ralph Lauren shirt, navy trousers, black belt and shoes. Sky-blue housekeeping uniform.

Faded black jeans, red bowling shoes, I ♥ NY T-shirt. Khaki pants, purple shirt, white tennis shoes. Khaki pants, rust-colored polo shirt. Khaki pants, yellow sweater, black shoes. Khaki pants, sage-green Izod shirt, Cole Haan shoes. Khaki pants, beige embroidered shirt, nylon knee-highs, brown moccasins. Khaki pants, green-striped long-sleeved Brooks Brothers shirt, boxer shorts, dark brown Timberland shoes with laces.

Samuel (Sandy) Ayala. He always thought he would die young. He believed he would not live past the age of thirty-six. In August 2001 he celebrated his thirty-sixth birthday.

B

Arlene T. Babakitis. Eustace P. (Rudy) Bacchus. John James Badagliacca. Jane Ellen Baeszler. Robert John Baierwalter.

American citizens from more than a hundred different countries of origin. Also citizens of Australia, Bangladesh, Belgium, Bermuda, Britain, Canada, China, Colombia, Ecuador, Egypt, France, Germany, Guyana, Indonesia, Ireland, Israel, Italy, Ivory Coast, Jamaica, Japan, Lebanon, Malaysia, Mexico, Moldova, the Netherlands, Peru, the Philippines, Portugal, Russia, South Africa, South Korea, Sweden, Switzerland, Taiwan, Ukraine, Venezuela, and Zimbabwe.

Andrew J. Bailey. Brett T. Bailey. Garnet Edward (Ace) Bailey.

The things they carried. Black briefcase containing a cell phone, a pager, and pictures of his son's first birthday party. Brown wallet in back pocket containing a scapular, a tiny red Bible, and a miraculous medal. Small black purse containing a sketchbook, a pen, and an alligator bottle opener. PalmPilot in aluminum hard case. Dog biscuits in pants pockets. Striped navy blue and silver backpack. Black briefcase containing a BMW magazine, the *Wall Street Journal,* literature about diabetes, a Sony Discman, CDs by Pink Floyd, the Ramones, and Depeche Mode. Three small statues of Buddha. Broken rosary in jacket pocket. Blood glucose meter, test strips, a bottle of insulin, and three disposable syringes.

Tatyana Bakalinskaya. Michael S. Baksh. Sharon M. Balkcom. Michael Andrew Bane. Kathryn Bantis. Gerard Jean Baptiste, firefighter, Ladder 9. **Walter Baran. Gerard A. Barbara,** firefighter, assistant chief, Citywide Tour Commander.

On Monday evening before he went to bed the pilot laid out his uniform just as he always did when he had an early-morning flight. He hung his freshly washed and ironed shirt from a knob on the armoire, pinned on the wings and the epaulets, put his ID in the pocket. He would be up before five in the morning. After showering and dressing quietly, he would kiss both his wife and his daughter on their foreheads without waking them. Then he would slip out the door. He would only be gone for two days.

Paul Vincent Barbaro. James William Barbella. Ivan Kyrillos Fairbanks Barbosa. Victor Daniel Barbosa. Christine J. Barbuto.

The Boeing 767 carries up to 255 passengers. It has a wingspan of 156 feet, 1 inch, and its overall length is 159 feet, 2 inches. Its maximum takeoff weight is 395,000 pounds. Its typical cruising speed is 530 mph. Its maximum fuel capacity is 23,980 gallons.

Colleen Ann Meehan Barkow. Her body was found on September 17, her first wedding anniversary.

David Michael Barkway. September 8 was his thirty-fourth birthday. Expectant father. His second child, a boy, was born on January 3, 2002.

Matthew E. Barnes, firefighter, Ladder 25. **Petty Officer Second Class Melissa Rose Barnes. Sheila Patricia Barnes. Evan J. Baron.**

The sound of a train whistle blowing through the city in the middle of the night was a potent wail of melancholy, an elongated echo of desire.

Renée L. Barrett-Arjune. Arthur Thaddeus Barry, firefighter, Ladder 15. **Diane G. Barry. Maurice Vincent Barry,** police officer, Port Authority.

What remains. Forty thousand baseball cards. Ten thousand postage stamps. Five thousand coins. Three thousand comic books. One thousand origami cranes. Eight hundred and fifty postcards. Seven hundred marbles. Six hundred and fifty bottles of fine wine. Six hundred matchbook covers. Five hundred and fifty antique die-cast model cars. Five hundred toys from McDonald's. Five hundred ceramic angels. Four hundred souvenir spoons. Three hundred cookbooks. Two hundred and fifty fridge magnets. Two hundred *Star Trek* videos. One hundred and fifty bayonets.

Scott D. Bart. On September 11, he had been married for five and a half weeks.

Carlton William Bartels. September 9 was his forty-fourth birthday.

Guy Barzvi. Inna B. Basina. Alysia Basmajian. Kenneth William Basnicki. Lieutenant Steven J. Bates, firefighter, Engine 235. **Paul James Battaglia. Walter David Bauer Jr.**

On Monday evening the senior flight attendant bought funny get-well cards for two of her colleagues who had called in sick, one with the flu and the other with strep throat. On Tuesday morning she mailed the cards from the airport before she got on the plane.

Ivhan Luis Carpio Bautista. September 11 was his twenty-fourth birthday.

Marlyn Capito Bautista. Mark Lawrence Bavis. Jasper Baxter.

All flight attendants had studied the instructions in the manual on how to handle a hijacking. Be persuasive to stay alive. Be released or escape. Delay. Maintain a professional role. Do not become an accomplice. Trust the law. Control other passengers and keep them occupied. Deter aggression. Serve food and nonalcoholic beverages. Use eye contact to encourage calmness and reduce anxiety. Learn and confirm the kind of weapon. Gather information. Be a good listener. Do not be a negotiator. After the hijacking, avoid the media. Debrief with authorized personnel.

Lorraine Grace Bay, flight attendant, United Airlines Flight 93. She had been on the job for thirty-seven years.

Michèle Du Berry Beale.

Frequent flier. The sales representative had made this trip so often now that he could have packed his overnight bag with his eyes closed. He had made this trip so often now that it was no more stressful than driving his car to work. He had made this trip so often now that he figured he could have flown the plane himself, also with his eyes closed.

Todd Beamer. Expectant father. His third child, a girl, was born on January 9, 2002.

Paul Frederick Beatini. September 14 was his tenth wedding anniversary.

Jane S. Beatty.

The things they had survived. Bladder cancer. Breast cancer. Colon cancer. Ovarian cancer. Prostate cancer. Thyroid cancer. Hodgkin's disease. Melanoma. Meningitis. Polio. Diabetes. Crohn's disease. Burst intestines. Ruptured spleen.

Kidney transplant. Quadruple heart bypass. Triple heart bypass. Hip replacement. Brain surgery for seizure disorder. Severe learning disabilities. Extreme panic disorder.

Alan A. Beaven. September 10 was his eighth wedding anniversary.

Lawrence Ira Beck. Manette Marie Beckles.

Tuesday morning. Running a little late, she had time to make the coffee and two pieces of toast, but then she only had time to eat one slice and drink half a cup. She left the mug and the plate on the table beside the birthday card she'd received from her mother yesterday. She brushed her teeth and fussed with her hair. She tossed papers and files into her briefcase. She located her keys in the jacket pocket of yesterday's suit. As soon as she got home from work, she'd clean up the kitchen and call her mom. But right now she had to run. She had a meeting first thing and she couldn't be late. She kissed her cat good-bye and, as usual, left the television tuned to CNN to keep him company while she was gone. She locked the door behind her and stepped into the sunlight.

Lieutenant Carl J. Bedigian, firefighter, Engine 214. He had once donated his bone marrow to save the life of a four-year-old boy he had never met. He had recently recovered from a rare condition that had left him paralyzed. On September 11, he had been married for less than one year.

Michael Ernest Beekman. María Asunción Behr.

Last seen wearing. Seiko watch with gold face, five strands of freshwater pearls. Brushed-gold wedding band with four channel-cut diamonds, Eddie Bauer watch with stainless-steel band. Silver ankle bracelet. Wooden cross on black wrist strap

with colored beads on either side. Platinum engagement ring with emerald-cut diamonds, platinum wedding band with four baguette diamonds, Calvin Klein watch with gray band, diamond pendant necklace. Small silver hoop earrings: three piercings in right ear, two in left. Movado white-gold watch on left wrist. Small gold angel pin on blouse.

Master Sergeant Max Beilke (retired). In 1973 he was the last American combat soldier to leave Vietnam.

Yelena (Helen) Belilovsky. Nina Patrice Bell. Debbie S. Attlas Bellows. Stephen Elliot Belson, firefighter, Ladder 24. **Paul Michael Benedetti. Denise Lenore Benedetto.**

Frequent flier. As of the beginning of September the salesman had logged just over one million lifetime miles in the air. He had spent so much time on airplanes that they'd become his home away from home, as comfortable and relaxing as his own living room. He had eaten so many airline meals that he had actually come to prefer them to home-cooked. He knew all the flight attendants' names, their spouses' names, their children's names, some of their personal problems, and a few of their fondest hopes and wildest dreams. Whenever he boarded yet another flight, he was greeted by the crew like a long-lost friend. He had spent so much time in the air, he often said, that he should be growing wings by now.

Bryan Craig Bennett. Eric L. Bennett. Oliver Duncan Bennett.

Still life. In the center of the kitchen table there was a wooden bowl of fruit: red apples, green grapes, three yellow pears. They were so flawless they did not look real. They were so pretty it did not seem right to eat them.

Margaret L. Benson. Dominick J. Berardi. James Patrick Berger. Steven Howard Berger. John P. Bergin, firefighter, Rescue 5. **Alvin Bergsohn. Daniel D. Bergstein.**

Moving. Making such a big change at her age was difficult, but she knew it was time. She could not face the prospect of another winter in New Jersey. She was going to live with her daughter in California. She had spent all summer dismantling her apartment, parceling out her belongings to friends, neighbors, and the needy. Eschewing all sentimentality, she had managed to distill her old life down to four suitcases and a box of jewelry. She had made copies of all her personal papers. She had even written her own obituary so there would be no mistakes when the time came. Her flight was Tuesday morning. She was ready to fly into the next chapter of her life.

Graham Andrew Berkeley. Michael J. Berkeley. Donna M. Bernaerts-Kearns. David W. Bernard. William H. Bernstein. David M. Berray. David Shelby Berry.

The dead rat lay flat on its back with its feet in the air. It was very fat with a very long tail. The young couple stepped out of the restaurant, laughing. Looking down at the sidewalk, suddenly the man groaned and cursed. The woman shrieked and covered her eyes. They ran away down the street like children and later they laughed at themselves, both born and raised here and still so squeamish about the wildlife.

Joseph John Berry. September 11 was his wife's fifty-fourth birthday.

William Reed Bethke. Yeneneh Betru. Timothy D. Betterly.

The sound of a train whistle blowing through the city in the middle of the night was an ardent invitation to adventure, a siren call to elsewhere.

Carolyn Beug. Daughter of **Mary Alice Wahlstrom,** also killed.

Edward Frank Beyea. Best friend of **Abraham J. Zelmanowitz,** also killed. Ed was a quadriplegic. Abe stayed with him after the attack.

Paul Michael Beyer, firefighter, Engine 6. **Anil Tahilram Bharvaney. Bella J. Bhukhan. Shimmy David Biegeleisen. Peter Alexander Bielfeld,** firefighter, Ladder 42. **William G. Biggart.**

At 8:21 a.m. American Airlines Flight 77, a Boeing 757, leaves Dulles Airport in Washington, D.C., bound for Los Angeles, California, with fifty-eight passengers and six crew members aboard.

Brian Bilcher, firefighter, Squad 1. On September 11, his first child, a boy, was two weeks old.

Mark K. Bingham. Carl Vincent Bini, firefighter, Rescue 5. **Gary Eugene Bird. Joshua David Birnbaum. George John Bishop.**

On Tuesday morning, sunshine filled the yellow kitchen. The extravagant bouquet of all white flowers (lilies, roses, gladioli, and freesia), a birthday present five days before, had dropped a few petals on the blue countertop during the night. The cats milled about, impatient for their breakfast. The dog stared meaningfully at the door. In the backyard birds were singing. On the radio there was music, news, and then the weather report: ebullient promises of a gorgeous day, currently 64°F, a predicted high of 80° with low humidity. The coffee brewed cheerfully while the bagels were toasting. The homemade blueberry jam was especially delicious.

Petty Officer Second Class Kris Romeo Bishundat. September 14 was his twenty-fourth birthday.

Jeffrey Donald Bittner. Balewa Albert Blackman Jr. Christopher Joseph Blackwell, firefighter, Rescue 3.

On Tuesday morning there was no milk, the orange juice was spilled, the baby was crying, the telephone kept ringing, he couldn't find his favorite shirt, an argument erupted over another unpaid parking ticket. The door was slammed and then he realized he had forgotten his briefcase. The door was slammed again and then he drove away. By the time he got to the end of the block he was sorry. As soon as he got to the office, he would call her and apologize.

Carrie R. Blagburn. Best friend of **Brenda Kegler,** also killed.

Susan Leigh Blair. Harry Blanding Jr. Janice Lee Blaney. Craig Michael Blass. Rita Blau. Richard Middleton Blood Jr. Michael Andrew Boccardi.

Bodies.

John Paul Bocchi. Michael Leopoldo Bocchino, firefighter, Battalion 48. **Susan Mary Bochino. Deora Frances Bodley.**

On Tuesday morning the husband and wife took the train together. They loved working in the same building. Once they arrived, they had coffee together in his office on the 88th floor, and then she went up to hers on the 93rd. After work they would meet in the lobby and take the train home again. Sometimes they fell asleep on the way, with their heads resting together and their hands clasped between them on the seat.

Bruce Douglas (Chappy) Boehm. September 11 was his nineteenth wedding anniversary.

Mary Catherine Murphy Boffa. Nicholas Andrew Bogdan. Darren Christopher Bohan. Lawrence Francis Boisseau. Vincent M. Boland Jr. Touran Hamzavi Bolourchi. Alan Bondarenko. André Bonheur Jr. Colin Arthur Bonnett. Frank J. Bonomo, firefighter, Engine 230. **Yvonne Lucia Bonomo.**

Distinguishing features: tattoos. Rose and sword on her left ankle, purple lilies across her lower back. Small bird on his upper right thigh. Butterfly on her upper left breast. Band of Celtic knotwork around his right bicep. Sword and dragon below her belly button. Sun with beaming rays on her right big toe, six-inch-wide black and purple tribal design on her lower back, from spine to hip. Bulldog head on his right shoulder with the number *58* on the dog tag. Dolphin, whale, and starfish on his left shoulder. Dragonfly on her back. Red and yellow Superman logo on his left arm. Celtic and Native American designs from her upper arms to her calves.

Sean Booker. Best friend of **Richard Lanard Allen,** also killed.

Kelly Ann Booms. Lieutenant Colonel Canfield D. Boone, posthumously promoted to colonel. **Mary Jane (M.J.) Booth. Sherry Ann Bordeaux.**

Tuesday morning. She was on vacation, but she went to work on Tuesday to fill in for a colleague. He was off that day, but he went down to the firehouse and got on the truck anyway. She had given her notice in August but agreed to stay on until a replacement could be found. He had worked there for one week of a one-month contract. She didn't work at the World Trade Center: she was only there to do some banking in the lobby. He was off that day, but he went down to the firehouse and got on the truck anyway. He had lost his job on Monday due to downsizing but went to the office on Tuesday morning to discuss his severance package. She got to work early on Tuesday, just as she always did. He didn't work at the World Trade Center: he was only there for a job interview. He was off that day, but he went down to the firehouse and got on the truck anyway.

Krystine C. Bordenabe. She was eight months pregnant with her second child.

Martin Michael Boryczewski. Richard Edward Bosco. Klaus Bothe.

Six men waiting for a train. They all lived in the same town and worked for the same company in the city. The most senior man had been there for twenty years, the most junior for just two weeks. They met up at the station every weekday morning at 6:25 to get to work by 8:30. Today they talked about the greatest cars they'd ever owned: a blue Datsun 240Z, a white 1965 Mustang convertible, a black Corvette Stingray, a red Sunbeam Tiger, a silver Porsche 911. The most junior man didn't say much: he hadn't owned a great car yet. He was mostly listening and observing, making mental notes, learning how to belong. The train pulled in. The men got on and found seats. Three read their newspapers and one read the Bible. The most senior man closed his eyes and went to sleep. The most junior man stared out the window and thought about great cars.

Carol Marie Bouchard. Friend of **Renée Lucille Newell,** also killed.

John Howard Boulton Jr. Francisco Eligio Bourdier.

Former lives. He used to be a firefighter, but then he became a stockbroker because it was safer and his wife wouldn't worry so much. He used to be an NYPD narcotics detective, but when his wife got pregnant he became a Port Authority officer instead because he thought it would be less risky. She used to be a police officer, but then she became a flight attendant because it was not so dangerous and she loved to travel. He used to be a stockbroker, but then he became a firefighter because it was more exciting and because, when you were a firefighter, you never had to wonder if what you did really mattered.

Thomas Harold Bowden Jr. On September 11, his second child, a girl, was twelve days old. She had been born two weeks early on August 31.

Donna Marie Bowen. Kimberly S. Bowers. Veronique Nicole (Ronnie) Bowers. Larry Bowman.

In the refrigerator, among other things, there were three yellow tomatoes and a large leafy head of Romaine lettuce. What had she been thinking, she wondered now, buying these perishable items the day before she left on her trip to California? As she locked the door, hoisted her suitcase into the trunk of the car, and headed for the airport, she wondered what the chances were that the vegetables would still be edible when she came home again a week from now.

Shawn Edward Bowman Jr. September 16 was his twenty-ninth birthday. Expectant father. His second child, a boy, was born on January 18, 2002.

Kevin L. Bowser. Gary R. Box, firefighter, Squad 1. **Gennady Boyarsky. Pamela J. Boyce.**

Tuesday morning. She was supposed to retire in the summer but had agreed to stay on until October to close out the fiscal year. He had just finished his shift, but he jumped on the fire truck and went anyway. He went to work early so he could help his mother later in the day. She didn't work at the World Trade Center: she was only waiting there for a bus. He had just finished his shift, but he jumped on the fire truck and went anyway. She went to work early so she could attend her son's first football game of the season later in the afternoon. He was working overtime, putting in an extra shift to help build up his pension. She didn't work at the World Trade Center: she was only there for a conference. He had just finished his shift, but he jumped on the fire truck and went anyway.

Allen P. Boyle. Expectant father. His third child, a boy, was born on November 21, 2001.

Michael Boyle, firefighter, Engine 33. Lifelong best friend of **David Gregory Arce,** firefighter, Engine 33, also killed. Their bodies were found together and buried side by side.

Alfred J. Braca. Sandra Jolane Conaty Brace. Kevin H. Bracken, firefighter, Engine 40.

Manhattan. Like most first-time visitors, she knew the facts. Manhattan: smallest by area of the five boroughs of Greater New York (the other four being the Bronx, Queens, Brooklyn, and Staten Island). Manhattan: the most densely populated borough, with 1.5 million people residing on an island thirteen miles long and slightly more than two miles across at its widest point. Manhattan: name derived from the Native American word *menatay,* meaning *island.* Manhattan: purchased by the Dutch from the Indians in 1626 for a box of trinkets worth about twenty-four dollars. Today this amount would buy less than one square inch of downtown office space. Like any first-time visitor, she was both exhilarated and overwhelmed. Clutching her guidebook like a small shield, she stepped off the curb and into the largest city in the country, fourth largest in the world.

Sandra W. Bradshaw, flight attendant, United Airlines Flight 93. September 21 was her son's first birthday.

David Brian Brady. Alexander Braginsky. Nicholas William Brandemarti.

At 8:35 a.m. the Federal Aviation Administration informs NORAD that American Airlines Flight 11 out of Boston has been hijacked.

Daniel Raymond Brandhorst-Gamboa. David Reed Brandhorst-Gamboa. Ronald Brandhorst-Gamboa. A family.

Michelle Renée Bratton. Patrice Braut. Lydia Estelle Bravo. Ronald Michael Breitweiser.

Baggage handler. Ballet dancer. Banker. Banquet and party planner. Banquet steward. Bartender. Battered women's shelter volunteer. Beverage manager. Billing supervisor. Biologist. Broadcast engineer. Broker. Budget analyst. Builder.

Edward A. Brennan III. Francis Henry Brennan. Michael Emmett Brennan, firefighter, Ladder 4.

Monday evening. After work they went grocery shopping, a chore they enjoyed doing together. They had the usual teasing skirmish over the man's penchant for buying the biggest of everything: forty-eight rolls of toilet paper, a hundred-pound bag of dog food, a whole case of canned tuna, a twelve-pack of toothpaste, a jar of sweet pickles the size and weight of a concrete block. He said it was more economical and besides, when the house was well-stocked with supplies, he felt they were ready for anything. She reminded him that there were just the two of them now, and they already had enough toilet paper to last for a year. And what exactly did they need to be ready for anyway? He just grinned and tossed a jumbo box of Cheerios into the cart.

Peter Brennan, firefighter, Rescue 4. Expectant father. His second child, a boy, was born on December 30, 2001.

Thomas M. Brennan. Expectant father. His second child, a boy, was born on October 24, 2001.

Captain Daniel J. Brethel, firefighter, Ladder 24. **Gary Lee Bright. Jonathan Eric Briley. Mark A. Brisman. Paul Gary Bristow. Marion Ruth Britton.**

Saturday morning at the market. Recently come from a small, simple town, the young woman went every week, counting this excursion as one of the great pleasures of city life. She took her time, browsing through the exotic fruits and vegetables as if they were books or blouses: celeriac, salsify, daikon, etrog, chayote, cherimoya, Israeli galia melons, limonera pears and blood oranges from Italy, passion fruit from Panama. She passed the potatoes from hand to hand: Delaware, spunta, sebago, Pontiac, estima, purple Congo, Yukon gold. She held jars of honey up to the light: clover, heather, orange blossom, French sunflower, Greek pine. Every Saturday she bought at least one thing she'd never tried before: crystallized rose petals, dried cape gooseberries, munthari and lemon myrtle chutney, a pomelo the size of a baby's head, six mauve plums called Tragedy, said to have a sweet sharp flesh.

Mark Francis Broderick. September 2 was his fortieth birthday.

Herman Charles Broghammer.

Tuesday morning. He was working overtime to make some extra money for his daughter's birthday present. He was off that day, but he went down to the firehouse and got on the truck anyway. She was working the early shift so she could pick up her daughter after her first day of school. He was off that day, but he went down to the firehouse and got on the truck anyway. She only worked in the office two days a week, Mondays and Tuesdays. He didn't work at the World Trade Center: he was only there for a trade show. She went to work early so she would have time later to prepare for her first night class in Advanced Microeconomics. He was off that day, but he went down to the firehouse and got on the truck anyway.

Keith A. Broomfield. He was the father of ten children.

Bernard Curtis Brown II. Janice Juloise Brown. Lloyd Stanford Brown. Captain Patrick J. Brown, firefighter, Ladder 3. **Bettina Browne-Radburn.**

Contingency plan. Once a year the insurance broker and his wife took a short vacation by themselves, leaving their three young children with one set of grandparents or the other for a week. Every year he insisted that he and his wife take separate flights so if there was a plane crash the children would not be orphaned. Sometimes his wife protested. She did not like traveling alone and she did not share his fatalism. She quoted the statistics proving that they were more likely to die driving together on the freeway than in a plane crash. But arguing accomplished nothing, and in the end she always went along with his plan just to keep the peace and humor him.

Mark J. Bruce. Richard George Bruehert. Andrew Christopher Brunn, firefighter, Ladder 5. **Captain Vincent Brunton,** firefighter, Ladder 105. **Ronald Paul Bucca,** FDNY fire marshal. **Brandon J. Buchanan.**

Gregory Joseph Buck, firefighter, Engine 201. **Dennis Buckley. Nancy Clare Bueche. Patrick Joseph Buhse.**

On the desk. Three photographs in silver frames. Christmas picture: husband and wife arm in arm, dressed up and smiling stiffly, with five children of varying sizes arranged around them. The smallest were twin girls with blond ringlets in identical red dresses in the foreground. The tallest was an almost-adolescent boy at the far right trying to look bored and manly in a green shirt and black tie. Summer picture: the wife standing in front of a concrete bridge over blue water, wearing a black bathing suit and a gold necklace and earrings, cradling a large silver fish in both hands. She was squinting into the sun, but the clouds above the bridge were ominous. Birthday picture: the twin girls in denim overalls and Disneyland T-shirts standing in front of an elaborate cake in the shape of an elephant with pink and yellow icing and five red candles.

John Edwards Bulaga Jr. On September 11, his second child, a girl, was four months old.

Stephen Bunin. Petty Officer Third Class Christopher Lee Burford. Matthew J. Burke.

At 8:42 a.m. United Airlines Flight 93, a Boeing 757, leaves Newark International Airport in New Jersey bound for San Francisco, California, with thirty-seven passengers and seven crew members aboard.

Thomas Daniel Burke. Lifelong friend of **James Lee Connor** and **John F. Iskyan,** also killed.

Captain William Francis Burke Jr., firefighter, Engine 21.

Bravery.

Captain Charles F. Burlingame III, pilot, American Airlines Flight 77. September 12 was his fifty-second birthday.

Thomas Edward Burnett Jr. Donald James Burns, firefighter, assistant chief, Citywide Tour Commander. **Kathleen Anne Burns. Keith James Burns.**

Broken.

John Patrick Burnside, firefighter, Ladder 20. **Irina Buslo.**

Favorite foods. Cotton candy. Fried cabbage. Pizza. Chicken cordon bleu. Shrimp cocktail. Stuffed peppers. Steak and cheese fries. Peach cobbler. Godiva chocolates. Grilled teriyaki beef. Ribollita. Oysters. Silver-dollar pancakes. Rice pudding. Peanut-butter pie. Sinigang soup. Macaroni and cheese. Crab cakes. Lamb chops. Lobster tails. Jerk chicken. Noodle kugel. Chocolate fondue. Rice Krispies squares. Strawberry milk. Marmite.

Milton G. Bustillo. On September 11, he had been married for twenty-five days. His first child, a girl, was seven months old.

Thomas M. Butler, firefighter, Squad 1. **Patrick D. Byrne,** firefighter, Ladder 101. **Timothy G. Byrne.**

The Boeing 757 carries up to 228 passengers. It has a wingspan of 124 feet, 10 inches, and its overall length is 155 feet, 3 inches. Its maximum takeoff weight is 255,000 pounds. Its maximum cruising speed is 600 mph. Its maximum fuel capacity is 11,489 gallons.

C

Petty Officer Third Class Daniel Martin Caballero. Jesus Neptali Cabezas. Lillian Caceres. Brian Joseph Cachia. Steven Dennis Cafiero Jr. Richard Michael Caggiano. Cecile Marcella Caguicla.

Last seen wearing. Red business suit. Tan business suit. Green business suit, tapestry blouse. Black pants, pink button-down shirt, herringbone tweed blazer, black wingtip shoes. White T-shirt and baggy blue jeans. Summer suit, blue-striped shirt, blue tie with white design. Suspenders with dark dress pants. Long white skirt, sleeveless tank top, black open-toed shoes, no stockings. Black skirt, white blouse, black bow tie. White shirt, gray pants, gray blazer with Port Authority logo. Dark pants and sweater, possibly cream-colored. Dark blue pants, sky-blue and white checked shirt, black shoes. Armani jeans and charcoal Prada shirt with suede collar. Dark olive or black slacks, olive-green short-sleeved shirt, white medium-sized Calvin Klein V-necked T-shirt, white Kenneth Cole briefs.

John Brett Cahill. Michael John Cahill. Scott Walter Cahill.

Tuesday morning. He went to work early to prepare for a special event. He had just finished his shift, but he jumped on the fire truck and went anyway. She had the flu, but she went to work despite her husband's protestations. He usually worked nights, but he took the breakfast shift to cover for a coworker. He went to work at dawn so he could make some calls to London and Tokyo and then be home by midafternoon. He had just finished his shift, but he jumped on the fire truck and went anyway. She was usually late for work, but on Tuesday she got there on time. He didn't work at the World Trade Center: he was only there for a meeting, a fact that he had forgotten to mention to his wife. He had just finished his shift, but he jumped on the fire truck and went anyway.

Thomas Joseph Cahill. September 14 was his thirty-seventh birthday.

George C. Cain, firefighter, Ladder 7. **Salvatore B. Calabro,** firefighter, Ladder 101. **Joseph M. Calandrillo. Philip V. Calcagno. Edward Calderon. Sergeant First Class José Orlando Calderón-Olmedo. Kenneth Marcus Caldwell. Dominick Enrico Calia. Felix (Bobby) Calixte. Captain Frank Callahan,** firefighter, Ladder 35.

Coming to America. Believing he would escape the poverty and violence that were destroying his own country. Here he liked the four distinct seasons, the tall buildings, the shiny stores, the plentiful food, the English language. Here, he had been told often enough, anything could happen. Here he thought he would be well dressed, well fed, well spoken, and safe.

Liam Callahan, police officer, Port Authority. September 12 was his twentieth wedding anniversary.

Suzanne M. Calley. September 12 was her twentieth wedding anniversary.

Luigi (Gene) Calvi. Roko Camaj.

Coming to America. As his family and the attendant responsibilities grew, he could see no other way. He had to make more money and he had to leave them behind to do it. He got work almost immediately. On the modest salary he earned as a security guard, he supported ten people back home: his wife and their four children, his parents and his three siblings. He called them every Sunday, budgeting carefully for the cost of the phone bill. He was lonely, but he knew it was worth it. He wouldn't have to live like this forever. He sent money home every paycheck, some of which they put away, saving to buy a piece of land and build a house when he, the hero of the whole village, finally returned.

Michael F. Cammarata, firefighter, Ladder 11. He died in the ninth week of a fourteen-week training program. His twenty-third birthday was on October 5, the day of his memorial service.

David Otey Campbell. Geoffrey Thomas Campbell.

Therapy. She went once a week, every Monday after work. Her therapist's office was tastefully decorated with leather furniture, glass-fronted bookcases, and some apparently expensive paintings of things she could not identify. They usually talked about the same productive (in the way a cough is said to be productive) topics: her father from whom she was estranged, her mother who had died suddenly ten years ago, her twin sister who thought she was the queen of the world. But this time they talked about something more specific: her fear of flying. Tomorrow she had to fly to Los Angeles. She already had a prescription for tranquilizers and was practicing deep-breathing relaxation techniques. Today her therapist was trying to convince her that her fears were completely unfounded.

Jill Marie Campbell. On September 11, her first child, a boy, was ten months old. That day he crawled for the first time.

Robert Arthur Campbell. Sandra Patricia Campbell.

On Tuesday afternoon the junior trader was going to summon up his courage and finally ask for that raise he thought he should have had six months ago.

Juan Ortega Campos. Sean Thomas Canavan. John A. Candela. Vincent A. Cangelosi. Stephen Jeffrey Cangialosi.

On Tuesday afternoon the event planner was going to tend to every single unanswered e-mail that had been languishing in her in-box for the last two weeks.

Lisa Bella Cannava. Sister of **John DiFato,** also killed.

Brian Cannizzaro, firefighter, Ladder 101. **Michael R. Canty. Louis Anthony Caporicci.**

On Tuesday afternoon the legal secretary was *definitely* going to finish that report she was supposed to have finished yesterday.

Jonathan Neff Cappello. His twenty-fourth birthday was on September 29, the day of his memorial service.

James Christopher Cappers. Richard Michael Caproni.

Cataclysm.

José Manuel Cardona. Expectant father. His second child, a boy, was born on January 2, 2002.

Dennis M. Carey, firefighter, Hazardous Materials Company 1. **Edward Carlino. Michael Scott Carlo,** firefighter, Engine 230. **David G. Carlone.**

The things they loved. He loved kayaking. She loved karate. He loved thoroughbred racing. She loved scuba diving. He loved snowboarding. She loved water-skiing. He loved tae kwon do. She loved whale watching. He loved weight lifting. She loved ballroom dancing. He loved opera. She loved baseball. He loved mountain climbing. She loved surfing. He loved skipping stones at the beach. She loved going to flea markets and tag sales. He loved playing Monopoly. She loved making gingerbread houses. He loved building birdhouses. She loved Abba. He loved Barbra Streisand. She loved the Beatles. He loved Jimi Hendrix, Led Zeppelin, Janis Joplin, and Pink Floyd.

Rosemarie C. Carlson. She was the mother of six children.

Mark Stephen Carney. Joyce Ann Carpeneto. Jeremy M. Carrington. Michael T. Carroll, firefighter, Ladder 3.

The things they hated. He hated cleaning the bathroom. She hated camping. He hated surprises. She hated vacuuming. He hated Christmas shopping. She hated writing letters. He hated shoveling snow. She hated crying. He hated sleeping alone. She hated baseball. He hated opera. She hated going to the dentist. He hated taking out the garbage. She hated her son's iguana. He hated hockey. She hated golf. He hated wearing a suit. She hated driving in the city. He hated SUVs. She hated flying. He hated country music. She hated Britney Spears.

Peter J. Carroll, firefighter, Squad 1. He was the father of six children.

James Joseph Carson Jr. Expectant father. His first child, a boy, was born on March 7, 2002.

Christoffer Mikael Carstanjen. Angelene C. Carter. James Marcel Cartier. Sharon A. Carver. Vivian Casalduc. John Francis Casazza. Paul Reegan Cascio.

Waiting at the gate to board the plane, at least five people were reading the same book. It was a weighty hardcover, almost six hundred pages. Not the usual choice of a book to carry while traveling, but such excitement had attended its publication that everyone wanted to read it right away. It was *The Corrections* by Jonathan Franzen, and it began this way:

The madness of an autumn prairie cold front coming through. You could feel it: something terrible was going to happen. The sun low in the sky, a minor light, a cooling star. Gust after gust of disorder. Trees restless, temperatures falling, the whole northern religion of things coming to an end.

Neilie Anne Heffernan Casey. On September 11, her first child, a girl, was six months old. September 21 was her fifth wedding anniversary.

William Joseph Cashman. Lifelong friend of **Patrick Joseph (Joe) Driscoll,** also killed.

Thomas Anthony Casoria, firefighter, Engine 22. He was to be married on October 13, 2001.

William Otto Caspar. Alejandro Castano. Arcelia (Chela) Castillo. Leonard M. Castrianno. José Raymod Castro. William E. Caswell.

At 8:43 a.m. the FAA informs NORAD that United Airlines Flight 175 out of Boston has been hijacked. Two F-15 fighter jets are scrambled from Otis Air National Guard Base at Falmouth, Massachusetts.

Richard G. Catarelli. Christopher Sean Caton. Robert John Caufield. Mary Teresa Caulfield.

In the air. Breakfast would be served shortly. There was a choice this morning between Belgian waffles with fruit and a ham-and-cheese omelet with home-fried potatoes. As usual, opinion on airline food was split: some people loved it and some people sneered at it. But by and large, most people would eat what they were given and then wait patiently or impatiently for more coffee.

Judson J. Cavalier. Best friend and roommate of **Joseph Peter Anchundia,** also killed.

Michael Joseph Cawley, firefighter, Ladder 136. **Jason David Cayne. Juan Armando Ceballos. Marcia G. Cecil-Carter. Jason Michael Cefalu. Thomas Joseph Celic. Ana Mercedes Centeno. Joni Cesta.**

A Knight's Tale. Once breakfast had been cleared away, the in-flight movie would be shown. It was described as a stylish, exciting, action-packed adventure set in the fourteenth century. Starring Heath Ledger, Mark Addy, Rufus Sewell, Alan Tudyk, and sensational newcomer Shannyn Sossamon. Ledger played William Thatcher, a peasant squire pretending to be a nobleman so he could become the world's jousting champion. *Hang on,* the promos said, *for the thrill ride of your life!* Some of the passengers were looking forward to the movie. Some had already seen it, so they would read instead or listen to one of the music channels on their headsets. Others would close their eyes and doze. A few would stare out the window at the clouds.

John J. Chada. September 13 was his fifty-sixth birthday.

Jeffrey Marc Chairnoff. Swarna Chalasini. William Chalcoff. Eli Chalouh. Charles Lawrence (Chip) Chan. Mei-ching (Mandy) Chang. Rosa Maria (Rosemary) Chapa. Mark Lawrence Charette. First Officer

David M. Charlebois, copilot, American Airlines Flight 77. **Gregorio Manuel Chávez.**

Chaos.

Delrose Eunice Forbes Cheatham. September 15 was her forty-ninth birthday.

Pedro Francisco Checo. Douglas MacMillan Cherry.

Whenever his father was away on a business trip, the boy had trouble sleeping. His mother tried to be patient. She sang to him, she read to him, she got him another glass of water. Eventually she was exhausted and fell asleep to the sound of the boy still crying into his pillow. In the morning she would find him asleep on the floor outside her bedroom door with his blanket, his teddy bear, and his thumb in his mouth.

Stephen Patrick Cherry. September 25 was his forty-second birthday.

Vernon Paul Cherry, firefighter, Ladder 118.

At 8:46:26 a.m. American Airlines Flight 11, traveling at an estimated 586 mph, crashes into the North Tower of the World Trade Center, Tower 1. It hits the building between floors 94 and 98, exploding with the force of 480,000 pounds of dynamite. The resulting fires burn at more than 1,800°F. The seismograph station at Palisades, New York, 21 miles north of Lower Manhattan, operated by the Lamont-Doherty Earth Observatory of Columbia University, registers the seismic equivalent of the impact at 0.9 on the Richter scale for a duration of 12 seconds.

Nestor Julio Chevalier. He was to be married in October 2001.

Swede Joseph Chevalier. Alexander H. Chiang.

Lucky. He considered himself lucky to have escaped the ax that had befallen his whole department. All but two employees had been let go on Friday afternoon, told to pack up their desks and never return. He was one of the lucky two who were spared. On Tuesday morning he straightened his tie, brushed the lint from his jacket, noted that he could use a haircut, and considered himself lucky to have a job to go to when all those other poor people had to stay home and figure out what to do next.

Dorothy J. Chiarchiaro. Aunt of **Dolores Marie Costa,** also killed.

Luis Alfonso Chimbo. Robert Chin. Wing Wai (Eddie) Ching. Nicholas Paul Chiofalo Jr., firefighter, Engine 235.

On Monday night they made love.

John G. Chipura, firefighter, Engine 219. He was to be married on October 27, 2001.

Peter A. Chirchirillo. Catherine Ellen Chirls. Kyung Hee (Casey) Cho.

For half an hour the young woman looked for the bracelet. It was her favorite, the one her father had given her when she graduated from college, the silver one with three small diamonds, small but sparkling, small but real. She knew he had worked many overtime hours to be able to afford the bracelet, not to mention to be able to send her to college in the first place. Finally she found it, tangled in the clothes in the bathroom hamper. She rushed out the door and ran down the street in her high heels. She made it to the corner stop just as the bus began to pull away. Luckily the driver saw her in his rearview mirror and put on the brakes. He grinned and opened the door again. She got on breathing hard, with her hair in disarray and the bracelet still clutched in her hand.

Abul K. Chowdhury. Best friend of **Nicholas Craig Lassman,** also killed. On September 11, he had been married for five months.

Mohammad Salahuddin Chowdhury. Expectant father. His second child, a boy, was born on September 13, 2001.

Kirsten Lail Christophe. September 13 was her daughter's first birthday.

Pamela Chu. Steven Paul Chucknick.

On the dining room table there was a half-finished jigsaw puzzle. It was not a picture of the Golden Gate Bridge, a German castle, a bucolic farm with chickens and cows, or a pair of fluffy white kittens playing with a ball of red wool. No. It was a 1952 Jackson Pollock painting called *Convergence,* and it was quite possibly, as the manufacturer claimed on the box, the world's most difficult jigsaw puzzle. Even the champion puzzler of the family could seldom place more than one or two pieces in an hour. He figured it would be a miracle if the puzzle was finished by Thanksgiving. His wife said it had better be because they were having twelve for turkey and there would be no room at the table for Jackson Pollock.

Wai-ching Chung. Uncle of **Maurita Tam,** also killed.

Christopher Ciafardini. Alex F. Ciccone. Frances Ann Cilente. Elaine Cillo. Edna Cintron. Nestor André Cintron III.

When the baby finally slept through the night for the first time, everyone was grateful. In the morning the whole family was exceptionally clear-eyed and cheerful.

Lieutenant Robert Dominick Cirri, police officer, Port Authority. He was the father of six children.

Juan Pablo Cisneros-Alvarez. Benjamin Keefe Clark. Eugene Clark. Gregory Alan Clark. Mannie Leroy Clark. Sarah M. Clark.

Café manager. Career consultant. Carpenter. CEO. Chairman. Chef. Chemist (retired). Chief engineer. Chief market analyst. Civil engineer. Claims analyst. Cleaner. Clerk. Clinical psychologist. Club manager. Communications representative. Comptroller. Computer consultant. Computer designer. Computer programmer. Congressional affairs liaison. Construction worker. Contractor. Cook. Corporate secretary. Courier. Court officer. Credit manager.

Thomas R. Clark. On September 11, his second child, a girl, was five months old.

Christopher Robert Clarke. On September 11, he had been married for six months.

Donna Marie Clarke. Michael J. Clarke, firefighter, Ladder 2. **Suria Rachel Emma Clarke.**

Conflagration.

Kevin Francis Cleary. James D. Cleere. Geoffrey W. Cloud. Susan Marie Clyne. Steven Coakley, firefighter, Engine 217. **Jeffrey Alan Coale. Patricia A. Cody.**

In the dream there were sirens and smoke and many people screaming. The young woman woke up sweating and gasping for breath with a bad taste in her mouth. It was her first time living away from home on her own, and right now she wished she'd never left. She was so frightened that she called her mother, twenty-five hundred miles to the west, where it was still light. Her mother, having just come in from the garden, said kindly, It was only a dream, dear. Go back to sleep now. Everything is fine.

Daniel Michael Coffey. Jason Matthew Coffey. Father and son.

Florence G. Cohen. Kevin Sanford Cohen. Anthony Joseph Coladonato.

Reasons to celebrate. They had found their dream home, a dramatic contemporary ranch house, and filled it with their collections of Mission-style furniture and modern art. They had been together for almost twenty years, longer and more happily than any of the straight couples they knew. Their families and friends said their names together as if they were one word. And now: a big promotion. They celebrated with a candlelit dinner of Chateaubriand and champagne. They stayed up all night talking. In the morning they had coffee on the patio, watching the dogs chase each other around the yard, admiring the rock garden, the lilies and the climbing roses, the white eggplants in the vegetable patch. Now, more than ever, they could not help but feel that their lives were lucky and charmed.

Mark Joseph Colaio. Stephen J. Colaio. Brothers. Mark was the brother-in-law of **Thomas E. Pedicini,** also killed.

Christopher M. Colasanti.

On Monday evening the office manager visited her father in the hospital, where he was slowly recovering from his third heart attack. She brought him some magazines and a crossword puzzle book. It looked like he was going to be in for a while yet.

Kevin Nathaniel Colbert. He and his girlfriend moved in together three weeks before.

Michel Paris Colbert.

At 8:50 a.m. the first FDNY trucks arrive at the World Trade Center. By 9:00 a.m. two hundred firefighters are on the scene.

Keith Eugene Coleman. Scott Thomas Coleman. Brothers.

Tarel Coleman, firefighter, Squad 252.

On Tuesday morning she left home early so she could vote in the primary before she went to work. The election was set to choose the candidates for a new mayor and other city officials. Having recently become more politically active, she and her brother had both been working as campaign volunteers for their favorite city council candidate. She was the third person to cast a vote that morning at the polling station in a nearby school. After she got to the office she called her brother, and they arranged to meet after work and spend the evening together watching the returns. With any luck, they would be going out later to celebrate.

Liam Joseph Colhoun. September 18 was his daughter's sixth birthday.

Robert Dana Colin. Robert Joseph Coll. Jean Marie Collin.

Amateur astronomer. Ever since he was a boy he had been intrigued by all things in the sky: stars, planets, moons, meteors, comets, and asteroids. When he was just eight years old his parents had given him a telescope for his birthday. That was the beginning. Now, forty years later, he had a den full of reference books and star maps, a high-powered computerized telescope in the backyard. On Tuesday morning the International Space Station was scheduled to pass directly overhead just before dawn. Both he and his wife were outside early, standing in the garden in their bathrobes, taking turns at the telescope, marveling at the vast beauty of the universe.

John Michael Collins, firefighter, Ladder 25. **Michael L. Collins. Thomas J. Collins. Joseph Collison.**

Secrets. He was an avid pro-wrestling fan and never missed the show: he knew this wasn't something he could or should tell just anyone. She had been dating the man at the next desk for three months: she hadn't told anyone yet because, after a dismal series of failed romances in recent years, she was afraid she would jinx it. He had been writing a novel for the past five years and now it was almost finished: he hadn't shown a word of it to anyone yet, but he was getting up his nerve to do just that. She suspected she was pregnant: she would go to the drugstore at lunch and buy the kit. She would do the test the next morning, and then she'd know for sure.

Jeffrey Dwayne Collman, flight attendant, American Airlines Flight 11. September 28 was his forty-second birthday.

Patricia Malia Colodner. Linda Migdalia Colon. Soledi E. Colon. Ronald Edward Comer. Jaime Concepción. Albert Conde. Denease Conley. Susan Clancy Conlon. Margaret Mary Conner. Cynthia Marie Lise Connolly.

Commuter hell. He had to drive two hundred miles back and forth to work every day, and he hated every minute of it. He figured he drove about fifty thousand miles a year, twice the total circumference of the earth. He had been doing this for six years. He could have driven around the world twelve times by now. Sometimes he couldn't remember why he was doing it. He knew he was sacrificing for the future but sometimes he couldn't remember what he had ever dreamed that future might hold.

John E. (Jack) Connolly Jr. September 27 was his fifteenth wedding anniversary.

James Lee Connor. Lifelong friend of **Thomas Daniel Burke** and **John F. Iskyan,** also killed.

Jonathan McManus (J. C.) Connors. Kevin Patrick Connors. Kevin Francis Conroy. Brenda E. Conway.

Early-morning indulgences. A bouquet of pink and purple asters with baby's breath from the street vendor in front of the towers who was there only on Tuesdays and Thursdays. A poppy-seed bagel and an iced cappuccino from the deli on the concourse level. The latest issue of *Vogue* to read at lunch. Juggling her purchases, her purse, and her briefcase, she got on the elevator and went up.

Dennis Michael Cook. On September 11, his second child, a girl, was four months old.

Helen D. Cook.

In recent weeks the elevators in the tower had not been operating properly. As if possessed by a willful and malicious spirit, they had taken to skipping floors, refusing to open and close, making strange squealing sounds, opening between floors, and often going unpredictably out of service for hours on end. And there was that persistent rumor that one had actually gone into free fall and been halted by the emergency brake just in the nick of time. Nobody seemed to know if this was really true or not, but the story continued to circulate with escalating embellishments each time it was retold.

Jeffrey W. Coombs. September 18 was his forty-third birthday.

John A. Cooper Jr. On September 11, his second child, a boy, was three months old.

Julian T. Cooper. Joseph John Coppo Jr. Gerard J. Coppola. Joseph Albert Corbett. John J. (Jay) Corcoran. Alejandro Cordero. Robert J. Cordice, firefighter, Squad 1. **Ruben D. Correa,** firefighter, Engine 74. **Danny A. Correa-Gutierrez. Georgine Rose Corrigan.**

Recovered: $230 million in gold and silver (379,036 troy ounces of gold and 29,942,619 troy ounces of silver) from the Bank of Nova Scotia vault under 4 World Trade Center.

Captain James J. Corrigan (retired), firefighter, Engine 320; head of fire and safety operations for the World Trade Center complex. His youngest son was married on September 8, 2001.

Carlos Cortes. Kevin M. Cosgrove.

On Monday afternoon she learned she had been granted the transfer to California that she had requested.

Dolores Marie Costa. Niece of **Dorothy J. Chiarchiaro,** also killed. September 13 was her fifty-third birthday.

Digna Alexandra Rivera Costanza. Charles Gregory Costello Jr. Michael S. Costello. Asia Cottom. Conrad K. H. Cottoy Sr. Martin John Coughlan. Sergeant John Gerard Coughlin, police officer, NYPD. **Timothy John Coughlin. James E. Cove. André Cox.**

Insomnia. In the dark bedroom there were so many things to worry about. Things that lined up quietly enough during the day, lurking patiently in the back of the mind, and then at midnight they swarmed forward with exuberance, fairly trampling each other in the ambush. The darkness grew heavy and fraught. The sheets were twisted like ropes. The pillows were damp and hot. The red numbers on the clock rolled relentlessly forward into morning. There was relief in the sunrise. There seemed nothing else to do then in the daylight but get up, get dressed, go to work, and get on with it. This was what most people did. For as long as they had to. Until the future finally arrived and rescued them.

Frederick John Cox. His girlfriend's older brother, **Davin Peterson,** was also killed.

James Raymond Coyle, firefighter, Ladder 3. **Michelle Coyle-Eulau.**

At 9:00 a.m. President George W. Bush is visiting Emma Booker Elementary School in Sarasota, Florida. National Security Adviser Condoleezza Rice informs him by telephone of the first plane crashing into the World Trade Center.

Anne Marie Martino Cramer. Christopher Seton Cramer. Formerly husband and wife.

Lieutenant Commander Eric Allen Cranford, posthumously promoted to commander. **Denise Elizabeth Crant.**

Courage.

James Leslie Crawford Jr. September 11 was his second wedding anniversary. Expectant father. His first child, a girl, was born in November 2001.

Robert James Crawford, firefighter, Safety Battalion 1. **Tara Kathleen Shea Creamer. Joanne Mary Cregan. Lucia Crifasi. Lieutenant John A. Crisci,** firefighter, Haz-Mat 1. **Daniel Hal Crisman. Dennis A. Cross,** firefighter, deputy chief, Battalion 57; posthumously promoted to battalion chief.

The things they carried. Black binder containing information about fighting high-rise fires. Nineteen seventy-six silver dollar in jacket pocket. Black duffel bag containing rope, gloves, water, and a can of tuna. Band-Aids in pants pockets. Brown briefcase containing *Sport Diver* magazine and the itinerary for a visit to New York planned by his mother but postponed. Three cell phones. Black wallet containing miniature copy of the Bill of Rights. Extra suitcase full of presents for their grandchildren. Sterling-silver money clip containing a Saint Christopher medal. Saxophone. Teddy bear. Five tickets to the September 12 game between the Yankees and the White Sox.

Helen P. Crossin-Kittle. On September 11, she had been married for five months. She was five months pregnant with her first child.

Kevin Raymond Crotty. Thomas G. Crotty. John R. Crowe. Welles Remy Crowther. Robert Lane Cruikshank.

On Monday evening they went to Lamaze class. The husband said he didn't see why they had to: they already had three children and surely they knew how to do this by now. The wife said a little refresher course couldn't hurt and besides, *she* was the one who would have to do all the hard work and actually *have* the baby, so he should just be quiet and come along happily. The husband had to admit she had a good point. He went outside and started the car.

John Robert Cruz. He became engaged two weeks before.

Kenneth John Cubas. Francisco Cruz Cubero. Thelma Cuccinello. Richard Joseph Cudina.

Lucky. The new husband considered himself lucky to have finally found a woman who did not ridicule his penchant for organization. She did not laugh when he rotated his clean socks and underwear in the drawer, putting those most recently washed in the back. She did not snort when he arranged his shirts in the closet by sleeve length, his pants by color, his shoes by season, and his sneakers by sport. She did not say a word when he spent one sleepless night color coding their address book. She did not even raise her eyebrows when he alphabetized all the spices and the canned goods in the pantry one Sunday afternoon when she was out. She had never once uttered the words *anal retentive* in his presence.

Neil James Cudmore. Fiancé of **Dinah Webster,** also killed.

Thomas Patrick Cullen III, firefighter, Squad 41.

Firehouse. New York's Bravest. Between fires, they stood around outside, chatting, joking, drinking coffee or Coke, lounging in the sunshine. They said hello to all the neighborhood residents who passed by, heading to work, to school, doing some shopping, some errands, walking their dogs, or just out for a stroll. And, of course, there were the pretty young women in their skimpy summer outfits for whom the men had their special smiles, maybe a wink, never a whistle, not anymore, such a thing no longer acceptable even here. Later they would go down to the corner grocery and flirt with the clerks, buy something to cook up for dinner, maybe help a pregnant woman or an elderly man carry their groceries to the car. For days now the men had seen little action and they were getting restless.

Joan McConnell Joudzevich Cullinan. She and her husband were in the process of adopting a child from China.

Joyce Cummings. Brian Thomas Cummins.

At 9:02:54 a.m. United Airlines Flight 175, traveling at about 480 mph, crashes into the South Tower of the World Trade Center, Tower 2. It hits the building between floors 78 and 84. The seismograph station at Palisades, New York, 21 miles north of Lower Manhattan, operated by the Lamont-Doherty Earth Observatory of Columbia University, registers the seismic equivalent of the impact at 0.7 on the Richter scale for a duration of 6 seconds.

Michael Joseph Cunningham. On September 11, his first child, a boy, was thirteen days old.

Robert Curatolo, firefighter, Ladder 16. On September 11, he had been married for three weeks.

Laurence Damian Curia. September 15 was his forty-second birthday.

Paul Dario Curioli. Patrick J. Currivan. Beverly LaVerne Crew Curry.

Washington, D.C. Like most new residents, he knew the facts. Situated on the northern banks of the Potomac River, covering an area of sixty-seven acres with a total metropolitan population of 5 million. Being a methodical person, once he got settled, he made a list and began to visit the city's famous landmarks. He had been to the Washington Monument, the Jefferson Memorial, Arlington National Cemetery, and the Lincoln Memorial. He had taken guided tours of the White House, the Capitol Building, the Library of Congress, the Smithsonian, the J. Edgar Hoover FBI Building, and the Pentagon. This weekend he was planning to visit the Vietnam War Memorial. Constructed in 1982. Polished black granite, 493.5 feet long and 10 feet high at its apex. Fifty-eight thousand names of the dead arranged chronologically, beginning with the first casualty in 1959 and ending with the last in 1975.

Sergeant Michael Sean Curtin, police officer, NYPD. September 11 was his wife's birthday.

Patricia Cushing. Sister-in-law of **Jane C. Folger,** also killed. This trip to California was Patricia's first flight on a commercial airplane. She was sixty-nine years old.

Gavin Cushny. He was to be married on October 26, 2001, the day he was buried.

D

John D'Allara, police officer, NYPD. **Vincent Gerard D'Amadeo. Jack L. D'Ambrosi. Mary Yolanda D'Antonio. Lieutenant Edward Alexander D'Atri,** firefighter, Squad 1.

Firehouse. Their coats hung on metal racks near the door: bulky black turnout coats with yellow and silver stripes on the sleeves, the chest, the bottom, their surnames in block yellow letters across the back. Their helmets were lined up on top of the racks. On the bottom shelves, their overalls sat just as they had stepped out of them after the last fire, with the boots still in them, ready to be stepped into again at the sound of the next alarm. One of the men had feet so big that when his new boots arrived they were packed in two separate boxes, one for each boot.

Michael D. D'Auria, firefighter, Engine 40. He had been on the job for eight weeks. The World Trade Center was his second fire.

Michael Jude D'Esposito.

Every morning when the billing supervisor went to work, she left her white cat sitting on the windowsill. He was deaf, arthritic, sixteen years old, safely marooned twenty stories up. But he was still watching the birds, still wishing he could fly. Every morning when she went to work, she had to admire him for that.

Caleb Arron Dack. September 29 was his eleventh wedding anniversary.

Carlos S. Dacosta.

Military honors. Purple Heart. Bronze Star. Legion of Merit. Army Commendation Medal. National Defense Service Medal. Sea Service Deployment Ribbon. Soldier's Medal for Heroism. Distinguished Flying Cross. Meritorious Unit Commendation. Defense Meritorious Service Medal. Navy and Marine Corps Achievement Medal. Armed Forces Expeditionary Medal. Good Conduct Medal. Joint Meritorious Unit Award. Coast Guard Special Operations Ribbon. Defense of Freedom Medal, awarded posthumously.

Captain Jason Dahl, pilot, United Airlines Flight 93. September 14 was his fifth wedding anniversary.

Brian Paul Dale. Thomas A. Damaskinos. Jeannine Marie Damiani-Jones.

Escape. One of these years she was going to treat herself to three days at the spa. She was going to partake liberally of the therapeutic pool, the cleansing sauna, and the soothing whirlpool. She was going to choose between the herbal body wrap, the milk-and-sesame stone wrap, and the peppermint-and-licorice wrap. She was going to have a Swedish massage, a Thai massage, or a Lomi Lomi Hawaiian massage, or maybe all three. She was going to finish off with the flower essence scalp treatment and a hydrating paraffin facial.

One of these years she was going to be completely transformed by a three-day escape to the spa, just as the brochure she kept in her top desk drawer so glowingly promised.

Manuel John DaMota. Best friend of **Obdulio Ruiz-Diaz,** also killed. Expectant father. His fourth child, a boy, was born on March 2, 2002.

Patrick W. Danahy. Expectant father. His third child, a girl, was born on October 11, 2001.

Vincent G. Danz, police officer, NYPD. **Dwight Donald Darcy. Elizabeth Ann Darling. Anette Andrea (Priya) Dataram.**

Reluctant visitor. She had never been to New York before. It had always scared her, just the idea of it: so big, so crowded, so noisy, so much violence, so much crime. She saw all this on television and read about it in the newspaper and that was more than enough. She had no desire to go there. But her company insisted she attend this one important meeting. She loved her job, her boss, her colleagues. She did not want to be difficult and she did not want to let anyone down. So she agreed. She arrived on Monday night. The taxi ride in from the airport was more than a little hair-raising, but she survived. The hotel was excellent, but she did not sleep well. The meeting was scheduled for nine o'clock in the morning on the 96th floor of the North Tower. She was up at dawn. She got there twenty minutes early.

Lawrence Davidson. Michael Allen Davidson. Scott Matthew Davidson, firefighter, Ladder 118.

Darkness.

Titus Davidson. He was the oldest son in a family of sixteen children.

Niurka Davila. Ada M. Davis.

Acrophobia. All his life he had been afraid of heights and now here he was working on the 103rd floor. He loved his job so much that he was willing to face the challenge of ascending in the elevator every morning, but he could not face the view. He always made sure he had an inside office, and whenever he had to pass the windows (so many windows!) he averted his eyes and walked as fast as he could despite the trembling that began in his legs, the sweat that sprang out on his brow, the nausea that rose in his stomach. Maybe someday he would get used to it. Maybe someday he would look down at the river and laugh.

Clinton Davis, police officer, Port Authority. Best friend of **Uhuru Gonja Houston,** police officer, Port Authority, also killed. Their bodies were found together.

Wayne Terrial Davis. Anthony Richard Dawson. Calvin Dawson. Edward James Day, firefighter, Ladder 11. **Ana Gloria Pocasangre de Barrera. Jayceryll M. de Chavez.**

On a hot summer Sunday afternoon he liked nothing better than to lie on the couch with a cold beer and listen to all his neighbors mowing their lawns. The sound was so soothing. After a while the smell of freshly cut grass filled the room and made him nostalgic for the easy suburban childhood he'd never had. As he dozed off, he promised himself (and his absent wife who was away for the weekend visiting her sister) that he would mow his own lawn after dinner when it was cooler.

Jennifer De Jesus. Monique E. De Jesus. Nereida De Jesus.

QVC. Quality. Value. Convenience. In other words, television shopping. When his wife was alive, she had enjoyed it immensely. Now she was gone and he did it alone, a guilty pleasure that seemed harmless enough, an innocuous way to pass a dreary afternoon, an empty evening, a solitary Sunday morning. Before he knew it, his apartment was filling up with things he never used and didn't need. Three elaborate juicers, two chrome-sided toasters, a pasta maker, a case of carpet shampoo, two dozen model cars, a BB gun, a cavalry sword, a chainsaw, two framed tickets to the 1969 Woodstock concert. What on earth was he going to do with all this stuff, he wondered, even as he contemplated the virtues of today's featured item: a fourteen-piece heavy-gauge tin-free steel nonstick bakeware set with three-tier cooling rack for under a hundred dollars.

Emerita (Emy) De La Peña. Best friend of **Judith Diaz-Sierra,** also killed.

Azucena María de la Torre. Francis Albert (Frank) De Martini.

The broken shutter banged all night in the wind. Every morning the bond broker meant to fix it, and every evening he forgot.

William Thomas Dean. Expectant father. His second child, a girl, was born on December 18, 2001.

Robert J. DeAngelis Jr. Thomas Patrick Deangelis, firefighter, chief, Battalion 8. **Dorothy Alma DeAraujo.**

Recovered: 65,000 personal items, including wallets, watches, jewelry, shoes, ID cards and badges.

Tara Moore Debek. On September 11, her first child, a girl, was six months old.

James Daniel Debeuneure.

MISSING. The poster was thumbtacked to the telephone pole at the corner. It featured a photograph of a small black-and-white dog of an indeterminate breed sitting on a red chair. *Last seen Friday afternoon.* The dog appeared to be smiling with his tongue hanging out. *Mongrel, two years old, about one foot tall, white bandage on left front leg, may be limping.* The sign was handwritten in block letters in black ink. *Wearing brown leather collar with silver name tag: LUCKY.* It had rained in the night, and the words at the bottom were blurry. *Much missed by children. . . . Reward offered. . . . Please call.*

Anna Marjia DeBin. Her eighth wedding anniversary was in September.

James Vincent DeBlase. Paul DeCola. Captain Gerald Francis Deconto. Simon Marash Dedvukaj.

On the tiny concrete balcony of the eighteenth-floor apartment there was a large gas barbecue with a black plastic cover, a silver mountain bike, a pair of yellow and blue downhill skis, a very healthy potted red geranium, a less successful herb garden in a terra-cotta planter. Sometimes laundry was hung to dry on the cast-iron railing. Every day the apartment's inhabitants talked about the house they were saving for: a *real* house with a chimney, a garage, dormers, and a big backyard. Meanwhile the still-life of objects on the balcony continued to proliferate.

Jason Christopher DeFazio. On September 11, he had been married for less than three months.

David E. Defeo. Manuel Del Valle Jr., firefighter, Engine 5; posthumously promoted to lieutenant. **Donald Arthur Delapenha. Vito Joseph DeLeo. Danielle Anne Delie. Andrea Della Bella. Joseph A. Della Pietra. Palmina Delli Gatti. Colleen Ann Deloughery.**

Despair.

Joseph Deluca. Boyfriend of **Linda Gronlund,** also killed. They were flying to California to celebrate her birthday.

Anthony Demas. Martin N. DeMeo, firefighter, Haz-Mat 1. **Francis Xavier Deming. Carol K. Demitz. Kevin Dennis. Thomas F. Dennis. Jean Caviasco DePalma. José Nicholas Depeña. Robert John Deraney. Michael DeRienzo. David Paul DeRubbio,** firefighter, Engine 226. **Jemal Legesse DeSantis. Christian Louis DeSimone.**

At 9:05 a.m. President Bush is sitting with a second-grade class at Emma Booker Elementary School when White House chief of staff Andrew Card informs him that a second plane has crashed into the World Trade Center. Card says, America is under attack.

Edward DeSimone III. September 15 was his thirty-seventh birthday.

Lieutenant Andrew J. Desperito, firefighter, Engine 1. September 25 was his nineteenth wedding anniversary.

Cindy Ann Deuel. Melanie Louise DeVere. Jerry DeVito. Robert Patrick Devitt Jr. Dennis Lawrence Devlin, firefighter, chief, Battalion 9. **Gerard P. Dewan,** firefighter, Ladder 3. **Sulemanali Ali Kassamali (Simon) Dhanani. Michael Louis DiAgostino.**

Data processing specialist. Defense department contractor. Delivery man. Designer. Director of information management. Disaster recovery specialist. Dishwasher. Draftsman. Driver. Drywall worker.

Matthew Diaz. His wife died of breast cancer in January 2002, leaving their two young sons to be raised by their grandmother.

Nancy Diaz. Michael A. Diaz-Piedra III.

Halloween had always been her favorite occasion. She was already planning this year's extravaganza. There would be cardboard gravestones all over the front yard and three fluorescent skeletons hanging from the trees. Skull-shaped lights would trim the porch, and the front door would be covered with cobwebs and bats. The stereo speakers would pipe scary music through the windows. Dressed as The Mummy (of course), she would stay home and give out the treats. Her husband, dressed as Frankenstein, would take the children around the neighborhood. Her five-year-old daughter wanted to be a fairy princess with wings and a sparkly wand. Her seven-year-old son wanted to be Count Dracula, with the teeth and the blood and everything. She was going to start making the costumes next week.

Judith Diaz-Sierra. Best friend of **Emerita (Emy) De La Peña,** also killed.

Patricia Florence DiChiaro. Rodney Dickens. Lieutenant Colonel Jerry Don Dickerson. Joseph Dermot Dickey Jr.

In the garden there were beans (green, yellow, lima), tomatoes (plum, cherry, beefsteak), cucumbers, carrots, cabbage, potatoes, squash, onions, garlic, and leeks. With varying degrees of success, he had tried growing eggplant, asparagus, celery, and cauliflower. One year he grew twenty-three varieties of lettuce. The next year he grew twelve different kinds of peppers. Last year he won the prize for biggest vegetable at the local fall fair for a pumpkin that weighed 103 pounds. He'd had his blue ribbon framed and hung it over the kitchen sink. He showed it to everyone who came to the house, including the UPS man and the meter reader.

Lawrence Patrick Dickinson. Brother-in-law of **Thomas G. Sullivan,** also killed. Expectant father. His second child, a boy, was born on December 4, 2001, his thirty-sixth birthday.

Michael David Diehl.

In the bathroom on top of the medicine cabinet there was a small glass vase filled with water and tiny colored stones. In the vase there were three stalks of bamboo, pale green, about ten inches tall, a little dusty on the leaves. The accompanying card said bamboo would bring good fortune for at least a year and that it would help align the flow of energy in the room. The card also said that three stalks of bamboo would bring happiness, five would bring health, and seven would bring unprecedented wealth.

John DiFato. Brother of **Lisa Bella Cannava,** also killed. September 9 was his twelfth wedding anniversary.

Vincent Francis DiFazio.

On Monday evening the mailroom manager registered for college, majoring in computer science.

Carl Anthony DiFranco. His wife had died on April 1, 2001, while waiting for a heart transplant. October 14 would have been their first wedding anniversary.

Donald J. DiFranco. Eddie A. Dillard. Deborann DiMartino. David DiMeglio. Stephen Patrick Dimino. William John Dimmling. Marisa DiNardo. Christopher M. Dincuff. Jeffrey Mark Dingle. Anthony Dionisio Jr.

The things they loved. She loved her husband's ears, which were small and delicate looking, of an unusual shape that always made her think of the lost city of Atlantis. He loved his wife's neck, which was slender and graceful, with a velvet shadow always nestled in the hollow at the base of her throat, that small marvel of the human body for which there must be a precise anatomical name but if there was one, he didn't want to know it, preferred to think of it as a nameless gift that pulsed beneath his fingers and tasted of salt and perfume.

George DiPasquale, firefighter, Ladder 2. September 12 was his ninth wedding anniversary. September 23 was his thirty-fourth birthday.

Joseph L. DiPilato. Douglas Frank DiStefano.

At 9:08 a.m. the FAA closes all airports in the New York City area.

Donald Americo DiTullio. Fiancé of **Natalie Janis Lasden,** also killed.

Ramzi A. Doany. Petty Officer First Class Johnnie Doctor Jr. John Joseph Doherty. Melissa C. Doi. Brendan Dolan. Captain Robert Edward Dolan Jr. Neil Matthew Dollard. James Joseph Domanico. Benilda Pascua Domingo.

Friday night, first date. The young man spilled his drink. The hamburger was so big he couldn't get his mouth around it. The special sauce dribbled down his chin. He got mustard on his sleeve. The young woman just smiled and handed him another paper napkin. She imagined that years later they would remember this night and laugh.

Alberto Dominguez. Charles (Carlos) Dominguez. Geronimo Mark Patrick (Jerome) Domínguez, police officer, NYPD.

Devastation.

Lieutenant Kevin W. Donnelly, firefighter, Ladder 3. **Jacqueline Donovan. Commander William Howard Donovan Jr. Stephen Scott Dorf. Thomas Dowd. Lieutenant Kevin Christopher Dowdell,** firefighter, Rescue 4. **Mary Yolanda Dowling. Raymond Mathew Downey,** firefighter, deputy chief, Special Operations; posthumously promoted to battalion chief.

Devotion.

Frank Joseph Doyle. His fourth wedding anniversary was in September.

Joseph Michael Doyle. Randall L. Drake.

At 9:21 a.m. the Port Authority of New York and New Jersey orders the closure of all bridges and tunnels in the New York City area.

Patrick Joseph (Joe) Driscoll. Lifelong friend of **William Joseph Cashman,** also killed.

Stephen Patrick Driscoll, police officer, NYPD. **Charles A. Droz III. Mirna A. Duarte. Luke A. Dudek. Christopher Michael Duffy. Gerard Duffy,** firefighter, Ladder 21.

Firehouse. The date, the shift, and the positions for both the Engine and the Ladder Truck were laid out in columns on the two house blackboards.

Officer	Officer
Chauffeur	Chauffeur
Nozzle	Outside Vent Man
Backup	Roof
Door	Irons
Standpipe	Can

The names of the men working that shift that day were printed in white chalk in the slots beside each position.

Michael Joseph Duffy. September 18 was his thirtieth birthday.

Thomas William Duffy. Antoinette Duger. Jackie Sayegh Duggan. Sareve Dukat.

Scripture. Each morning before she left her apartment, the waitress opened the Bible and studied a short passage, most often a few verses from one of the Psalms, which was her favorite book. On Tuesday morning she considered a portion of Psalm 91:

You will not fear the terror of the night, or the arrow that flies by day, or the pestilence that stalks in darkness, or the destruction that wastes at noonday.

A thousand may fall at your side, ten thousand at your right hand, but it will not come near you.

She left the Bible open on her pillow and headed off to work.

Commander Patrick S. Dunn. Expectant father. His first child, a girl, was born on March 15, 2002.

Christopher Joseph Dunne. Richard Anthony Dunstan. Patrick Thomas Dwyer.

A decision. It was beginning to feel more and more like the right thing to do. He had been thinking about it for months, waffling mostly, talking himself into and out of it with equal frequency and conviction. But now he was almost ready. They had been dating for seven years and they weren't getting any younger. Next month, he decided. Next month he would do it. She had often said October was her favorite month. So yes, in October he would definitely do it.

In October he would ask her to marry him.

E

Joseph Anthony Eacobacci. John Bruce Eagleson. Petty Officer First Class Edward Thomas Earhart. Robert Douglas Eaton.

Emptiness.

Dean Phillip Eberling. September 11 was his daughter's tenth birthday.

Margaret Ruth Echtermann. Paul Robert Eckna. Constantine (Gus) Economos. Barbara G. Edwards. Dennis Michael Edwards. Michael Hardy Edwards. Captain Martin Joseph Egan Jr., firefighter, Division 15.

At 9:24 a.m. the FAA informs NORAD that American Airlines Flight 77 out of Washington has been hijacked. Two F-16 fighter jets are scrambled from Langley Air Force Base in Virginia.

Christine Egan. Michael Egan. Sister and brother.

Lisa Egan. Samantha Martin Egan. Sisters.

Carole B. Eggert. Lisa Caren Weinstein Ehrlich. John Ernst (Jack) Eichler. Eric Adam Eisenberg. Daphne Ferlinda Elder. Michael J. Elferis, firefighter, Engine 22. **Mark Joseph Ellis,** police officer, NYPD. **Valerie Silver Ellis.**

Editorial director. Electrical engineer. Electrician. Electronics technician. Elementary school student. Elevator operator. Environmental engineer. Environmental lawyer. Epidemiologist. Event planner. Executive assistant. Executive television producer.

Albert William (Alfy) Elmarry. Expectant father. His first child, a girl, was born on April 4, 2002.

Lieutenant Commander Robert Randolph Elseth. Edgar Hendericks Emery Jr. Doris Suk-Yuen Eng. Christopher S. Epps. Ulf Ramm Ericson. Erwin L. Erker.

Gifts. Although his wife's thirtieth birthday wasn't until the end of September, he had already bought her presents. They were all wrapped in shiny paper with ribbons and bows, hidden on the top shelf of a cupboard in the basement, stashed behind a cordless drill and three half-empty cans of paint. He had bought her a hand-painted blue and green silk scarf, a leather-bound journal made in Italy, and a pair of black pearl earrings set in twenty-four-carat gold. He had also ordered, from the Internet, a long-out-of-print almost-impossible-to-find book of photographs of Egypt, her ancestral homeland, which they planned to visit next year. He just hoped the book would arrive in time for her birthday.

William John Erwin. On September 11, his first child, a boy, was almost three months old.

Sarah Ali Escarcega. José Espinal. Fanny G. Espinoza. Brigitte Ann Esposito.

A fish story. Most weekends, spring, summer, and fall, he went fishing with his three older brothers. They dreamed collectively of someday landing a fifty-pound striped bass. They would have it stuffed and mounted on a wooden plaque engraved with the weight and the date. Then they would share it, each man hanging it in his own house for three months of the year. In this fantasy all of their wives loved having a big dead fish prominently displayed in the living room.

Francis Esposito, firefighter, Engine 235. **Lieutenant Michael A. Esposito,** firefighter, Squad 1; posthumously promoted to captain. Cousins.

William Esposito. September 16 was his twenty-ninth wedding anniversary.

Ruben Esquilin Jr. Sadie Ette. Barbara G. Etzold. Eric Brian Evans. Robert Edward Evans, firefighter, Engine 33.

Eternity.

F

Catherine K. Fagan. Patricia Mary Fagan. Keith George Fairben, paramedic.

Distinguishing features. Vertical scar from cesarean section. Large mole on his left shoulder, one-inch scar from his hairline to the middle of his forehead. Surgical scars on both her cheekbones, rosacea and skin discoloration on her neck. Cyst on his forehead above the right eyebrow. Gap between her front teeth. Malformed left thumb, tumor behind his right ear. Six feet, six inches tall; size sixteen shoe. Left breast removed. Deaf. Skin graft on abdomen, tip of his right thumb missing. Rod in her spine, beauty marks all over. Pierced nipples. Purple contact lenses. Scars from severe burns on his arms, legs, stomach, and back. Moon-shaped birthmark on her right calf, pierced belly button. Bite mark on his chest just below the left shoulder.

Charles S. Falkenberg. Dana Falkenberg. Leslie A. Whittington Falkenberg. Zoe Falkenberg. A family.

Petty Officer Third Class Jamie Lynn Fallon. William F. Fallon. William Lawrence Fallon Jr. Anthony J. Fallone Jr. Dolores Brigitte Fanelli. Robert John Fangman, flight attendant, United Airlines Flight 175.

At 9:26 a.m., for the first time in history, the FAA orders all nonmilitary airplanes grounded. All flights into, out of, and within the United States are canceled. There are more than forty-five hundred flights in the air at this time.

John Joseph (Jack) Fanning, firefighter, battalion chief, Haz-Mat Operations. He was the father of two autistic children.

Kathleen Anne (Kit) Faragher. Captain Thomas J. Farino, firefighter, Engine 26; posthumously promoted to battalion chief. **Nancy Carole Farley.**

The bus stop was directly across the street from an eight-story yellow-brick apartment building. Each morning a row of pigeons perched along the edge of the roof. Each morning, waiting there for the bus to work, the accountant counted the birds: nine, eleven, eighteen, twenty-three, twenty-six, thirty. She read the row of pigeons like tarot cards or her daily horoscope: an ornithological teller of fortunes. The higher the number of birds, she imagined, the better her day would be. She had always put her faith in numbers.

Paige Marie Farley-Hackel. Best friend of **Ruth Magdaline Clifford McCourt** and her daughter **Juliana Valentine McCourt,** also killed.

Elizabeth Ann (Betty) Farmer. Douglas Jon Farnum. John Gerard Farrell. John William Farrell.

To-do list. Sometimes he made it late at night sitting at the kitchen table with one small lamp burning and the wall-clock ticking like a pulse into the silent room. Sometimes he made it in the morning standing at the kitchen counter while the coffee brewed and his wife fed the baby. Either way he always tucked it into his breast pocket before he left for work, patting it as he kissed his family good-bye. He could not imagine getting through the day without his list.

Pick up dry cleaning.
Call exterminator.
Get new watch strap.
Make appointment for tune-up.
Research air conditioners.
Buy milk.
Order flowers.
Call mother.

Terrence Patrick Farrell, firefighter, Rescue 4. He had once donated his bone marrow to save the life of a young girl suffering from T-cell lymphoma.

Captain Joseph D. Farrelly, firefighter, Division 1; posthumously promoted to battalion chief. **Thomas Patrick Farrelly. Syed Abdul Fatha. Christopher Edward Faughnan. Wendy R. Faulkner. Shannon Marie Fava.**

On the desk there was a picture of a baby in a ceramic frame featuring a bunch of balloons, red, green, and blue. The baby stared steadfastly into the camera with big brown eyes. Wisps of dark hair escaped from beneath a knitted blue hat. In the lower right corner there was one small hand in a matching blue mitten with a penguin on it. Beside the photograph there was a coffee mug that said *World's Best Grandma!* in excited red letters. Beside the mug, a bowl of red and white strawberry candies for anybody who happened to stop by.

Bernard D. Favuzza. September 11 was his fifty-second birthday.

Robert Fazio Jr., police officer, NYPD. **Ronald Carl Fazio.**

Field trip to the Channel Islands off the coast of California. Three students, three teachers, and two representatives from the National Geographic Society flying from Washington, D.C., to Los Angeles on Tuesday morning. The children were well prepared. They had their brochures in their backpacks. They had studied all the information and the photographs before they left. They knew they were going to see kelp beds, tide pools, rugged canyons, and dramatic steep cliffs. They might see blue and humpback whales, sea lions, brown pelicans, and elephant seals. They knew that many of these species were endangered. They had promised not to get too close to any of the animals and frighten them. They had promised to behave themselves on the airplane, too. So far they were doing a good job but they were so excited that already it was getting harder and harder to sit still.

Chief William M. Feehan, firefighter, first deputy commissioner. At seventy-one, he was the oldest and highest-ranking firefighter ever to die in the line of duty.

Francis Jude (Frank) Feely. Garth Erin Feeney. Sean B. Fegan.

Cities. Two years ago a trip to Istanbul. Mosques, minarets, the muezzin's call to prayer. The Gate of Salutation, the Harem, the Treasury, where she saw two eight-pound uncut emeralds and an eighty-four-carat diamond, the Sacred Column, which was said to weep water that could work miracles. Two years before that, Venice. Canals, gondolas, piazzas, palazzi. The Rialto Bridge, the Campanile di San Marco, the Galleria dell'Accademia, where she saw paintings by Bellini, Titian, and Tintoretto. Just this past summer, two whole weeks in Paris. She would be picking up the photos this afternoon, all ten rolls of them. She used to say that once she got to see Paris, then she could die happy. But already she was thinking about the next trip: Athens, London, Vienna, Madrid? The possibilities were endless.

Lee S. Fehling, firefighter, Engine 235. Expectant father. His second child, a girl, was born on October 18, 2001.

Peter Adam Feidelberg. Meredith Emily June Ewart Feidelberg. Husband and wife. They were married in March 2000 and had renewed their vows in a second wedding ceremony on August 11, 2001.

Alan D. Feinberg, firefighter, Battalion 9. **Rosa Maria Feliciano. Edward Porter Felt. Edward Thomas Fergus Jr. George J. Ferguson. James Joe Ferguson.**

At 9:30 a.m. President Bush, still at Emma Booker Elementary School in Sarasota, Florida, makes his first official comments on the tragedy. He says, Terrorism against our nation will not stand. He asks for a moment of silence. He says, May God bless the victims, the families, and America.

Henry Fernandez. Judy Hazel Fernandez. Julio Fernandez.

Not-done-yet list. She kept it in her Daytimer at the end of the current month, moving it ever forward as the ensuing months inevitably arrived. During the course of any given month she could usually check two or three things off this master list, but then there were always three or four more things to be added and so the list continued to grow.

Clean oven.
Paint bedroom.
Renew passport.
Clean out basement.
Have outdoor receptacle installed.
Have fridge serviced.
Reorganize kitchen cupboards.
Mend bathroom curtains.
Clean out hall closet.
Will.

Elisa Giselle Ferraina. Anne Marie Sallerin Ferreira. Robert John Ferris. David Francis Ferrugio. Louis V. Fersini Jr. Michael David Ferugio. Bradley James Fetchet. Jennifer Louise Fialko. Kristen Nicole Fiedel.

Faith.

Amelia Virginia Fields. September 11 was her forty-sixth birthday.

Samuel Fields. Expectant father. His fifth child, a boy, was born on February 11, 2002.

Alexander Milan Filipov. September 14 was his forty-fourth wedding anniversary.

Michael Bradley Finnegan. Timothy J. Finnerty. Michael Curtis Fiore, firefighter, Rescue 5. **Stephen J. Fiorelli Sr.**

Exercise. Every night he ran four miles. He even ran in the winter and came home with icicles in his hair. If the neighbors happened to be outside shoveling snow when he ran past, they just waved and shook their heads. He had the body of a much younger man, and he was justifiably proud of it. At his annual physical in July, two weeks after his fiftieth birthday, his doctor congratulated him on taking such good care of himself. The doctor, who was a jovial sort, said, I wouldn't be surprised if you live to be a hundred.

Paul M. Fiori. On September 11, his second child, a girl, was three months old.

John B. Fiorito. Lieutenant John R. Fischer, firefighter, Ladder 20; posthumously promoted to captain. **Andrew Fisher. Bennett Lawson Fisher. Gerald Paul (Geep) Fisher.**

Recovered: 19,858 body parts.

John Roger Fisher. He was the father of seven children.

Thomas Joseph Fisher.

At 9:30 a.m. the New York Stock Exchange is evacuated, and trading is suspended.

Lucy A. Fishman. September 9 was her sixth wedding anniversary.

Ryan Daniel Fitzgerald. Thomas James Fitzpatrick. Richard P. Fitzsimons.

Fashion buyer. File clerk. Filmmaker. Finance manager. Financial adviser. Floor-covering installer. Food and beverage controller. Food preparer. Food runner. Food-service handler. Food-service manager. Forensic accountant. Former combat photographer. Former FBI counterterrorism agent. Former professional hockey player. Freelance commercial producer.

Salvatore A. Fiumefreddo. His first wedding anniversary was on September 29, the day of his memorial service.

Wilson (Bud) Flagg. Darlene (Dee) Flagg. Husband and wife.

Christina Donovan Flannery. On September 11, she had been married for three months.

Eileen Flecha. Fiancée of **Ivan Perez,** also killed.

Andre G. Fletcher, firefighter, Rescue 5; posthumously promoted to fire marshal. **Carl M. Flickinger. Petty Officer Second Class Matthew Michael Flocco. John Joseph Florio,** firefighter, Engine 214. **Joseph Walkden Flounders. Carol Ann Flyzik. David Lawrence William Fodor. Lieutenant Michael N. Fodor,** firefighter, Squad 1. **Stephen Mark Fogel. Thomas Foley,** firefighter, Rescue 3.

Falling.

Jane C. Folger. Sister-in-law of **Patricia Cushing,** also killed.

David J. Fontana, firefighter, Squad 1; posthumously promoted to lieutenant. September 11 was his eighth wedding anniversary. His thirty-eighth birthday was on October 17, the day of his memorial service.

Chih Min (Dennis) Foo. Godwin Forde. Donald A. Foreman, police officer, Port Authority. **Christopher Hugh Forsythe.**

Former lives. After fifteen years of active navy service, he was posted to the Pentagon. His family was relieved because now they didn't have to worry every day that his ship would be attacked or bombed or torpedoed or otherwise sunk in some faraway sea. His family figured the Pentagon must be the safest place in the world. Plus now he would be home for dinner every night, not to mention Thanksgiving, Christmas, Easter, and everybody's birthday.

Claudia Alicia Martinez Foster. Noel John Foster. Sandra N. Foster. Ana Fosteris.

The things they had survived. Homelessness. Alcoholism. Heroin addiction. Prison. Rape. Internment in a German displacement camp during World War II. The Gulf War. The Korean War. The Vietnam War. The 1993 bombing of the World Trade Center, in which six people were killed and more than a thousand were injured.

Robert Joseph Foti, firefighter, Ladder 7. On September 11, he had been married for four months.

Jeffrey L. Fox. Virginia Fox. Virgin Lucille (Lucy) Francis. Gary Jay Frank. Morton H. Frank.

Forsaken.

Peter Christopher Frank. He was to be married on October 19, 2001.

Colleen Laura Fraser. Richard K. Fraser.

Favorite books. *Ulysses. Don Quixote. War and Peace. The Iliad. Moby-Dick. The Adventures of Marco Polo. The Catcher in the Rye. Faust. Being and Time. The Cat in the Hat. Green Eggs and Ham. Harry Potter and the Chamber of Secrets. The Lord of the Rings. How to Make Money Buying and Selling Houses. The Andromeda Strain. The Other Side of Midnight. Angela's Ashes.*

Kevin Joseph Frawley. September 11 was his one-month wedding anniversary.

Clyde Frazier Jr. Lillian Inez Frederick. Andrew A. Fredericks, firefighter, Squad 18; posthumously promoted to lieutenant. **Tamitha Freeman. Brett Owen Freiman. Lieutenant Peter L. Freund,** firefighter, Engine 55. **Arlene Eva Fried. Alan Wayne Friedlander. Andrew Keith Friedman.**

Fragment, *noun.*

1. A broken off, detached, or incomplete part.
2. A comparatively small detached portion; a broken piece.
3. A part remaining when the rest is lost or destroyed.

Paul J. Friedman. In May 2001 he and his wife adopted a baby boy from Korea.

Gregg J. Froehner, police officer, Port Authority. **Lisa Anne Frost. Peter Christian Fry.**

When the baby crawled for the first time, he went clear across the kitchen and on into the dining room. There was much applause and picture taking.

Clement A. Fumando. His thirty-ninth wedding anniversary was on September 30, the day of his memorial service.

Steven Elliot Furman. September 13 was his forty-first birthday.

Paul James Furmato. September 19 was his fourteenth wedding anniversary.

Karleton D. B. Fyfe. Expectant father. On September 9, his wife found out she was pregnant with their second child. The baby, a boy, was born on May 18, 2002.

G

Fredric Neal Gabler. Expectant father. His first child, a girl, was born on November 9, 2001.

Richard P. Gabriel. Richard Samuel Frederick Gabrielle. James Andrew Gadiel. Pamela Lee Gaff. Ervin Vincent Gailliard.

Traffic. It was Friday afternoon and they were stuck. Their yellow cab was surrounded. Bumper to bumper, mirror to mirror, they could not move. Behind them someone kept stupidly blasting his horn, as if that would do any good. But they did not get excited. They were used to it, they had expected it, they were resigned. They remained calm, their cab driver, too. He pulled out his cell phone and began talking in a foreign language, animated and cheerful. They promptly did the same, the three of them chatting happily enough into their little plastic phones while all around them the toxic traffic stewed. A siren blared urgently behind them, and they tried not to think about the fact that this ambulance, police car, or fire truck couldn't possibly get through this jam and at the other end someone was waiting to be rescued, desperate or dying.

Deanna Lynn Micciulli Galante. Grace Catherine Galante. Cousins by marriage. Deanna was seven months pregnant with her first child. She had been married for seven and a half weeks.

Anthony Edward Gallagher. Daniel James Gallagher.

The things they carried. Turquoise woven shoulder bag containing prescription sunglasses in a quilted cloth holder, a journal with red leather cover and two ribbon bookmarks, a library copy of *Gone with the Wind,* one New York bagel in a Ziploc bag. Black leather wallet containing two laminated four-leaf clovers and one condom. Orange and gray Northface backpack. Large silver key ring with twenty-five keys. BlackBerry 5810. Navy blue gym bag containing red Nike shorts, white T-shirt, clean socks and underwear, green towel, shampoo, deodorant, *Runner's World* magazine. Two tickets for September 12 flight to Puerto Rico.

John Patrick Gallagher. On September 11, his first child, a boy, was two months old.

Lourdes Galletti. Cono E. Gallo. Vincenzo (Vincent) Gallucci. Thomas Edward Galvin. Giovanna Galletta (Genni) Gambale. Thomas Gambino Jr., firefighter, Rescue 3. **Giann Franco Gamboa. Peter J. Ganci,** firefighter, chief of FDNY.

Firehouse. They washed and polished the trucks every day. They also polished the fire poles. They inventoried the tools and equipment: flashlights, axes, sledgehammers, pike hooks, closet hooks, extension hooks, chainsaws, disc saws, sawzalls, ring cutters, respirators, resuscitators, blankets, searchlights, and medical kits. They cleaned and checked the apparatus: hoses, nozzles, ladders, pumps, ropes, wedges, blocks and tackle, acetylene torches for cutting through steel, all kinds of extinguishers, including the Purple K for airplane fuel fires.

Claude Michael Gann. On September 11, he had been married for two months.

Lieutenant Charles William Garbarini, firefighter, Battalion 9.

Firehouse. They teased each other about who had been chosen (or not chosen) for the 2002 *Firehouse Hunks* calendar. They gave each other bad haircuts. They played practical jokes on the probies: peanut butter or shaving cream smeared on the telephone receiver, fridge door handles and hinges switched, a water-filled balloon above the bathroom door. They worked out in the weight room. One of them could benchpress 455 pounds and the others all hoped to beat that someday. They bragged about their recent performances with the softball and basketball teams. They reminisced about the annual ski races, five men to a team, clinging to the fire hose, riding it down the mountain. They plotted their strategy for the next charity lacrosse game against their archrivals, the NYPD, who could not be allowed to win again this year.

Andrew Garcia. Cesar R. Garcia. David Garcia. Juan Garcia. Marlyn del Carmen Garcia. Christopher S. Gardner.

On the bedside table there was a glass of water, a scented candle, a small box of Kleenex, and a stack of poetry books. On the top was *Homecoming* by Julia Alvarez and on the bottom, *Ararat* and *The Wild Iris* by Louise Glück. In between there were books by Maya Angelou, Emily Dickinson, Rita Dove, Sharon Olds, and Sandra Cisneros. In the drawer of the table there was a silver pen and a green leather-bound notebook. More than half its pages were filled with lines written in a tidy delicate hand. Each poem was titled in elegant calligraphic script, and at the end of each was the date, one poem a day for the last three months.

Douglas Benjamin Gardner. September 11 was his father's birthday.

Harvey Joseph Gardner III. Jeffrey Brian Gardner. Thomas A. Gardner, firefighter, Haz-Mat 1. **William Arthur Gardner.**

At 9:32 a.m. all financial markets in the United States are closed. They do not reopen until the following Monday, September 17. The markets have not been closed for three consecutive workdays in eighty-seven years, not since 1914 during World War I, when they were closed for four months.

Francesco (Frank) Garfi. Rocco Nino Gargano.

On Monday evening they went bowling.

James Michael Gartenberg. Expectant father. His second child, a girl, was born on March 11, 2002.

Matthew David Garvey, firefighter, Squad 1. **Bruce H. Gary,** firefighter, Engine 40. **Boyd Alan Gatton.**

Painting. If it hadn't been for his daughter talking him into taking an evening class with her two years ago, he might never have discovered that not only did he love watercolor painting, but he was good at it, too. His daughter stopped painting once the class was over, but he set up a studio for himself in the spare room. He spent an hour or two there every evening after dinner, and now he'd done well over a hundred paintings. Apples, pumpkins, sailboats, houses, shops, a birdcage, a rose bush, three white lilies in a white vase against a black backdrop. Occasionally he dreamed of showing his paintings in public someday, but mostly he was happy just giving them as gifts to family and friends. He looked forward to his impending retirement: then he could take some more classes and spend more time in the studio.

Donald Richard Gavagan Jr. Expectant father. His third child, a boy, was born on October 23, 2001.

Peter Alan Gay. Terence D. Gazzani. Gary P. Geidel, firefighter, Rescue 1. **Paul Hamilton Geier. Julie M. Geis. Peter Gerard Gelinas. Steven Paul Geller. Howard G. Gelling Jr.**

Piano lessons. When she was a young girl she'd wanted very badly to learn how to play the piano like her two best friends did. She felt left out when they practiced and when they talked about the new pieces they were learning. But her mother said lessons were a luxury they couldn't afford. A few years later there was more money, but then her mother said there was no room in the house for a piano. For many more years after that she forgot all about it, but now the woman who'd just moved in next door turned out to be a piano teacher. So here she was, nearly fifty years old, and her first lesson was scheduled for next Wednesday evening, and she was already shopping for a piano.

Peter Victor Genco Jr. On September 11, his second child, a girl, was three months old.

Steven Gregory Genovese. Alayne F. Gentul.

The woman in the yellow dress leaned against the railing of the ferry. The wind swirled her skirt around her legs and blew her hair across her face. The sun sparked off the surface of the water. The woman shielded her eyes and brushed her hair away from her mouth. She was pale and thin. The city drew closer. She picked up her briefcase from where it rested at her feet, turned her back on the view, squared her shoulders, and sighed. Another day at the office. If only she could ride back and forth on the ferry all day instead, just watching the sun go placidly through its paces.

Linda M. George. She was to be married on October 20, 2001.

Edward F. Geraghty, firefighter, deputy chief, Battalion 9; posthumously promoted to battalion chief. **Suzanne Geraty.**

On Monday evening the architect visited his mother in the nursing home. Although her Alzheimer's was advanced now and she no longer knew who he was, still she seemed to enjoy his company.

Ralph Gerhardt. Boyfriend of **Linda Anne Luzzicone,** also killed.

Robert J. Gerlich. Denis P. Germain, firefighter, Ladder 2. **Marina Romanovna Gertsberg. Susan M. Getzendanner. Captain Lawrence Daniel Getzfred. James Gerard Geyer. Cortez Ghee. Joseph M. Giaccone.**

At 9:38 a.m. American Airlines Flight 77 crashes into the southwest wing of the Pentagon. The fighter jets from Langley are still 105 miles, or 12 minutes, away. This is the first successful direct attack on Washington, D.C., since the War of 1812.

Lieutenant Vincent Francis Giammona, firefighter, Ladder 5; posthumously promoted to captain. September 11 was his fortieth birthday.

Debra Lynn Fischer Gibbon.

At the museum. He went as often as he could, at least once a week, more often if he could manage it. He went to be quiet. He went to be still. He went to forget about his career and his frustrated ambition, his loneliness and his unrequited love, his mother's mental illness and his father's sudden death. He went to look at the same painting for an hour. Raphael: *Madonna and Child Enthroned with Saints;* the Virgin's pale serene face, her red and black robes, the plump baby on her knee. El Greco: *View of Toledo;* the lowering sky, the melancholy hillside, the distant gray spire of the cathedral. Vermeer: *Young Woman with a Water Pitcher;* her white headdress, the half-open leaded window, the brass pitcher, the map on the wall behind her, and the light, of course, the light. He went to forget about himself for an hour, then he went back to work.

James Andrew Giberson, firefighter, Ladder 35. On September 5, he celebrated his twentieth anniversary with the FDNY.

Brenda C. Gibson. Craig Neil Gibson. Ronnie E. Gies, firefighter, Squad 288; posthumously promoted to lieutenant.

Bedtime. She turned off the television and locked the doors. She turned off the lights and went upstairs. She put on her nightgown, washed her face, and applied the expensive new moisturizer that promised to combat the seven signs of aging. She brushed her teeth and thought about flossing but didn't. She tiptoed into her son's bedroom. She picked up the teddy bear that had either fallen or been tossed to the floor. She nestled it back in beside him and made the sign of the cross over them both. She went into her bedroom, closed the drapes, and got into the empty bed. Her husband was working the graveyard shift and wouldn't be home until morning. She would be glad when he was back on days.

Andrew Clive Gilbert. Timothy Paul Gilbert. Brothers.

Paul Stuart Gilbey. Paul John Gill, firefighter, Engine 54. **Mark Y. Gilles. Evan Hunter Gillette. Ronald Lawrence Gilligan. Sergeant Rodney C. Gillis,** police officer, NYPD. **Laura Gilly. Lieutenant John F. Ginley,** firefighter, Engine 40.

Gone.

Donna Marie Giordano. Jeffrey John Giordano, firefighter, Ladder 3. **John J. Giordano,** firefighter, Engine 37. **Steven A. Giorgetti.**

Gravity.

Martin Giovinazzo Jr. Best friend of **Steven Leon Howell,** also killed.

Kum-Kum (Kim) Girolamo. Salvatore Gitto. Cynthia Giugliano. Mon Gjonbalaj.

The Pentagon, headquarters of the United States Department of Defense (army, navy, and air force), covers an area of 29 acres with a total of 6.6 million square feet of floor space. Of that, 3.7 million square feet is office space, housing approximately 23,000 employees, both military and civilian. The building contains 7,754 windows, 691 water fountains, 284 restrooms, 131 stairways, 19 escalators, and 13 elevators. Although it contains 17.5 miles of corridors, it takes a maximum of only seven minutes to walk between any two points in the building. Construction began on September 11, 1941, and was completed on January 15, 1943.

Dianne Gladstone. Best friend of **Diane Maria Urban,** also killed.

Keith Alexander Glascoe, firefighter, Ladder 21. Expectant father. His third child, a boy, was born on April 30, 2002.

Thomas Irwin Glasser. Edmund Glazer. Harry Glenn. Barry H. Glick.

The things they loved. He loved riding rodeo bulls. She loved in-line skating. He loved wreck diving. She loved family reunions. He loved chopping wood. She loved being a foster parent. He loved being a Cub Scout leader. She loved watching fireflies in the backyard. He loved playing Uno and Crazy Eights with his children. She loved playing Trivial Pursuit. He loved coaching his son's basketball team. She loved teasing her brother. He loved doing birdcalls. She loved the Boston Celtics. He loved the Green Bay Packers. She loved the Westminster Dog Show. He loved gumball machines. She loved John Lennon. He loved clamming. She loved flower arranging. He loved cowboy boots. She loved reading the tabloids. He loved whittling. She loved the painted houses of San Francisco. He loved the lighthouses of Maine. She loved John Belushi. He loved playing goalie for the restaurant soccer team. She loved the Chicago Bulls and Michael Jordan. He loved Manchester United and British beer.

Jeremy Glick. September 3 was his thirty-first birthday. On September 11, his first child, a girl, was three months old.

Steven Lawrence Glick. John T. Gnazzo. William Robert Godshalk. Michael Gogliormella. Brian Fredric Goldberg. Jeffrey Grant Goldflam. Michelle Herman Goldstein. Monica Goldstein. Steven Goldstein. Colonel Ronald F. Golinski (retired). Andrew H. Golkin.

The things they hated. She hated the way her husband always left the wet towels in a heap on the bathroom floor after he showered, and if she complained about it, he just grinned and said he wouldn't do it again, but he *did* do it again the very next morning. He hated the way his wife suddenly felt compelled to vacuum the living room just when he had settled in to watch the game on Sunday afternoon. She hated the way her son drank the milk right out of the carton, standing there with the fridge door open, and if he happened to empty the carton, he would put it back in the fridge anyway.

Dennis James Gomes. September 3 was his first wedding anniversary. On September 11, his first child, a girl, was six months old.

Enrique Antonio Gomez. José Bienvenido Gomez. Brothers.

Manuel Gomez Jr. Wilder Alfredo Gomez.

Genealogist. General property manager. General's aide. Graduate student. Grill cook.

Jenine Nicole Gonzalez. Mauricio Gonzalez. Rosa Julia Gonzalez.

Last seen wearing. Ebel platinum watch, wedding band engraved *9/9/95,* double heart ring on her right hand engraved *L&G,* Peretti heart necklace from Tiffany's. Gold crucifix on gold chain. Black Citizen watch with orange button and black band. Square aquamarine ring, gold ring with small gold snake. Silver necklace with doughnut-shaped jade charm. Two-tone Rolex watch with blue face. Gold signet ring engraved with family crest: a fist holding a crescent moon on a black stone. Gold and blue enamel medal of the Virgin Mary.

Lynn Catherine Goodchild. Girlfriend of **Shawn M. Nassaney,** also killed. They were traveling to Maui for a four-day vacation before returning to college.

Calvin J. Gooding. Expectant father. His second child, a girl, was born on October 23, 2001.

Peter Morgan Goodrich. Harry Goody III. Kiran Reddy Gopu. Catherine Carmen Gorayeb. Lisa Reinhart Fenn Gordenstein. Kerene Gordon. Sebastian Gorki.

Secrets. He had been employed by the Defense Department for many years, but his work was so classified that he could not tell his family much about what he did every day. He made frequent trips from Boston to Los Angeles, but he could not say why. Sometimes he couldn't even say where he was staying or exactly how long he would be gone. His wife and children had learned not to ask too many questions. Whenever another trip came up, they simply helped him pack, wished him a safe journey, and kissed him good-bye.

Kieran Joseph Gorman. Expectant father. His third child, a boy, was born in October 2001.

Thomas Edward Gorman, police officer, Port Authority. **Michael Edward Gould. Douglas Alan Gowell. Yuji Goya. Jon Richard Grabowski. Christopher Michael Grady. Edwin John Graf III. David Martin Graifman. Gilbert Franco Granados.**

On the bulletin board above the kitchen telephone. A receipt from the American Cancer Society for a donation in the amount of fifteen dollars. A receipt from Macy's for a white silk blouse that didn't fit right after all and needed to be returned. A receipt from Blockbuster Video for the rental of *The Story of Us* and *The Sixth Sense,* both due back on Wednesday by midnight. A reminder notice from the vet, the dog being slightly overdue for his shots. A reminder notice from the Toyota dealership, the car being seriously overdue for a tune-up. A card with the address of their polling station for the September 11 primary. A long list of names and phone numbers. A short list of emergency phone numbers. A detailed list of complete dinner menus for the next two weeks.

Lauren Catuzzi Grandcolas. She was two months pregnant with her first child.

Elvira Granitto. Winston Arthur Grant.

Dream house. They knew when they bought the old house that it would be a lot of work, but they were not daunted. They were committed. They were in the throes of renovations for three solid years. Sanding and refinishing the hardwood floors; installing new kitchen cabinets, a skylight in the bedroom, new plumbing, new wiring, a second bathroom, new windows up and down; moving a wall and then moving it back; painting, painting, so much painting. For three years they inhaled sawdust, paint fumes, and polyurethane. For three years they tripped over tools, cords, and drop cloths. On Saturday, September 8, the last tile was grouted, the last door was hung, even the front porch had been sanded and repainted, and finally it was finished. Every little thing: done. They popped the champagne cork and filled their glasses.

Christopher Stewart Gray. Ian J. Gray. James Michael Gray, firefighter, Ladder 20. **Linda Catherine Mair Grayling.**

Recovered: 437 watches.

John Michael Grazioso. Timothy George Grazioso. Brothers.

Andrew Peter Charles Curry Green. Derrick Arthur Green. Wade Brian Green. Wanda Anita Green, flight attendant, United Airlines Flight 93. **Elaine Myra Greenberg. Donald F. Greene. Gayle R. Greene. James Arthur Greenleaf Jr. Eileen Marsha Greenstein.**

Going to the cemetery on Sunday afternoon. His mother had died of breast cancer five years ago. Now he went every week to visit her grave. In the fall he planted red and orange chrysanthemums at the headstone. Once the ground had thawed in the spring, he put in dozens of tulip bulbs. When the tulips were finished, he replaced them with a carpet of pink and white impatiens. After he had tended to the flowers, he liked to wander around a bit. It was an old cemetery, and many of the dates engraved on the lichen-covered headstones were from the 1800s. He liked to imagine the stories buried beneath them. His favorite was not a headstone at all, but a small flat square of granite surrounded by grass.

It had no dates, no place names, no comforting words from the Bible chiseled across the bottom. It didn't even have a surname on it. All it said, in plain block letters, was *Jack and Honey.*

Elizabeth (Lisa) Martin Gregg. Denise-Marie Alethia Gregory. Donald H. Gregory. Florence Moran Gregory.

Favorite movies. *Casablanca. Camelot. Forrest Gump. How the Grinch Stole Christmas. Braveheart. Ghostbusters. Gladiator. You've Got Mail. Harold and Maude. Thelma and Louise. In the Line of Fire. The Godfather. The Matrix. The Blues Brothers. The Wild Bunch. The Wizard of Oz.*

Pedro (David) Grehan. John Michael Griffin. Tawanna Sherry Griffin. Joan Donna Griffith. Warren Grifka. Ramon Grijalvo. Joseph F. Grillo. David Joseph Grimner. The Reverend Francis Edward Grogan.

On the kitchen calendar: September. *Septembre. Settembre. Septiembre.*

The picture: *Musician Angels,* detail from *Coronation of the Virgin* by Fra Angelico. Oil on wood, 213 x 211 cm. Musée du Louvre, Paris. Eight angels with blond curls, brown eyes, rosebud lips, gold embossed halos like plates. Robes of red, blue, green, and pink decorated with gold embroidery. One playing the lute, two blowing long gold trumpets with their cheeks puffed out like chipmunks.

Below the picture, the grid of the month with the days of the week in five languages: Sunday. *Sonntag. Dimanche. Domenica. Domingo.* Monday. *Montag. Lundi. Lunedì. Lunes.* Tuesday. *Dienstag. Mardi. Martedì. Martes.*

Linda Gronlund. Girlfriend of **Joseph Deluca,** also killed. September 13 was her forty-seventh birthday. They were flying to California for a celebratory vacation.

Kenneth George Grouzalis. Joseph Grzelak, firefighter, chief, Battalion 48.

On the kitchen calendar: September. *Septembre. Settembre. Septiembre.*

Four squares marked with printed information in a typeface so tiny it called for a magnifying glass. September 3: Labor Day (Canada, USA). September 17: Rosh Hashanah (begins at sundown). September 22: Autumnal Equinox (23:04 Greenwich Mean Time). September 26: Yom Kippur (begins at sundown).

Five other squares marked with personal details in very neat handwriting in black ink. September 5: Doctor, 3:30 p.m. September 10: Haircut, 4:15 p.m. September 15: Dad's birthday. September 21: House insurance due.
September 27: Sonogram, 2:50 p.m.

Matthew James Grzymalski. Boyfriend of **Kaleen Elizabeth Pezzuti,** also killed.

Robert Joseph Gschaar. Liming (Michael) Gu. Richard Jerry Guadagno. José Antonio Guadalupe, firefighter, Engine 54. **Yan Zhu (Cindy) Guan. Lieutenant Geoffrey E. Guja,** firefighter, Battalion 43.

Ground Zero, *phrase.*

1. The ground directly below the point of detonation of a nuclear weapon.
2. *Colloquially,* the very beginning, the starting point.

Lieutenant Joseph P. Gullickson, firefighter, Ladder 101. September 28 was his fifth wedding anniversary.

Babita Girjamatie Guman. Douglas Brian Gurian. Janet Ruth Gustafson. Philip T. Guza. Barbara Guzzardo. Peter Mark Gyulavary.

Distinguishing features: tattoos. Cross and roses on his right forearm, with the inscription *In Memory of Mom 11/30/89.* Heart on her neck, with husband's name, *Justin.* Sun symbol on his right ankle. Heart on her right hand between thumb and index finger. Grim Reaper on his upper right arm. Grateful Dead on his left ankle. Shamrock on his left forearm. Oak tree with four large branches on his arm. Wife's name, *Sally,* on one arm; dragon entwined with FDNY emblem on the other. Logo of Emerald Society Pipes and Drums Band on his calf; family crest on upper right arm, with the inscription *Death Before Shame* in Gaelic.

H

Gary Robert Haag. Andrea Lyn Haberman. Barbara Mary Contarino Habib. Philip Haentzler. Nezam Ahmad Hafiz. Karen Elizabeth Hagerty. Steven Michael Hagis Jr. Mary Lou Hague. David Halderman Jr., firefighter, Squad 18; posthumously promoted to lieutenant. **Maile Rachel Hale. Diane M. Hale-McKinzy.**

At 9:45 a.m. the White House is evacuated.

Richard B. Hall. Stanley R. Hall. Vaswald George Hall. Robert John Halligan.

Weather. In the winter she hated the cold and the snow. She preferred to stay inside, where it was warm. In the summer she hated the heat and the humidity. She preferred to stay inside, where it was air-conditioned. In the spring and the autumn she hated the rain. She preferred to stay inside, where it was dry. She was not an outdoor person.

Lieutenant Vincent Gerard Halloran, firefighter, Ladder 8. Expectant father. His sixth child, a girl, was born on May 17, 2002, his wedding anniversary.

Carolyn B. Halmon. James Douglas Halvorson. Mohammad Salman Hamdani. Felicia Hamilton. Robert Hamilton, firefighter, Squad 41.

Carl Max Hammond Jr. Frederic Kim Han. Christopher James Hanley. Sean S. Hanley, firefighter, Ladder 20. **Valerie Joan Hanna. Thomas Hannafin,** firefighter, Ladder 5.

The joy of cooking. On Saturday she shopped for the ingredients and on Sunday she spent the whole day in the kitchen. She was in her glory chopping, mixing, blanching, and sautéing. Each Sunday friends came over for dinner and marveled at her creations. She wrote down all her recipes in a thick notebook, now tattered and spotted with grease, and sometimes she took pictures of the new dishes before they were devoured. She could think of nothing more pleasurable and satisfying than watching the people she loved eat the food she had prepared for them. This week she had a new idea involving pork chops, apples, and walnuts. She could hardly wait to try it out.

Kevin James Hannaford. Expectant father. His second child, a boy, was born on January 9, 2002.

Michael Lawrence Hannan. Dana R. Hannon, firefighter, Engine 26.

Hell.

Christine Lee Hanson. Peter Burton Hanson. Susan Kim Hanson. A family. Christine was the youngest person to die on September 11. She was two years old.

Vassilios G. Haramis. James A. Haran. Gerald Francis Hardacre. Jeffrey Pike Hardy. Timothy John (T. J.) Hargrave. Daniel Edward Harlin, firefighter, Ladder 2. **Frances Haros.**

Heroes.

Lieutenant Harvey L. Harrell, firefighter, Rescue 5. **Lieutenant Stephen Gary Harrell,** firefighter, Battalion 7. Brothers. September 18 was Harvey's eighteenth wedding anniversary.

Aisha Anne Harris. Girlfriend of **Curtis Terrence Noel,** also killed.

Stewart Dennis Harris. John Patrick Hart. Eric Samadikan Hartono. John Clinton Hartz. Emeric J. (Ric) Harvey.

Favorite movies. *The Cutting Edge. The Sound of Music. The Ten Commandments. Breakfast at Tiffany's. Sleepless in Seattle. Star Wars. X-Men. Batman. Dr. Strangelove. Wall Street. Philadelphia. When Harry Met Sally. On Golden Pond. Doctor Zhivago. The Good, the Bad, and the Ugly. It's a Wonderful Life. Apocalypse Now.*

Sara Elizabeth Manley Harvey. September 11 was her one-month wedding anniversary.

Peter Paul Hashem.

Honor.

Thomas Theodore Haskell Jr., firefighter, battalion chief, Division 15. **Timothy Haskell,** firefighter, Squad 18. Brothers.

Joseph John Hasson III. On September 11, his first child, a boy, was almost three months old.

Leonard William Hatton Jr., volunteer firefighter, special FBI agent.

At 9:48 a.m. the Capitol Building is evacuated and all other federal buildings in Washington, D.C., are closed.

Captain Terence S. Hatton, firefighter, Rescue 1. Expectant father. On September 12, his wife found out she was pregnant with their first child.

Michael Helmut Haub, firefighter, Ladder 4.

The things they had survived. He was shot in the left shoulder during an armed robbery; his arm was sewn back on in three subsequent operations. He was shot on three different occasions in the line of duty. He was shot in the spine. He was shot in both legs when stepping out of a phone booth.

Timothy Aaron Haviland. Brother-in-law of **Robert W. Spear Jr.,** firefighter, Engine 50, also killed.

Donald G. Havlish Jr. Anthony Hawkins. Nobuhiro Hayatsu. James Edward Hayden.

Favorite foods. Lemon meringue pie. Marinara sauce. Collard greens with kale and turnip. Bouillabaise. Lechon. Gefilte fish. French fries and gravy. Chocolate soufflé. Grilled-cheese sandwiches. Lemon chicken. Buffalo wings. Filet mignon, medium rare. Prime rib and Yorkshire pudding. Yellow and green squash with onions. Empanadas. Oxtail soup. Belgian waffles. Girl Scout cookies. Pickled herring. Meatloaf. Salmon. Pinangat. Orange roasted chicken. Horseradish. Strawberry shortcake. Reese's Peanut Butter Cups.

Philip Thomas Hayes, firefighter (retired), Engine 217. He was the second oldest of sixteen children.

Robert Jay Hayes. On September 11, his second child, a boy, was five months old.

William Ward Haynes. Scott Jordan Hazelcorn. Lieutenant Michael K. Healey, firefighter, Squad 41. **Roberta Bernstein Heber. Charles Francis Xavier Heeran.**

Walking to the park on Sunday afternoon. The father carried the little girl on his shoulders, her blue sandals bumping against his chest. The mother pushed the little boy in his stroller, handing him apple slices from a plastic bag, some of which he ate and the rest he threw on the ground, laughing. He was briefly afraid of a barking black Lab lunging toward him, but he only cried for a minute and the dog ran on. Shirtless teenage boys played Frisbee. Three old women all in black, even their stockings black in the heat, sat in a row on a white park bench. There was a man making balloon animals: a giraffe for the girl, a rabbit for the boy. They played on the swings and the small slide. Then they had chocolate ice-cream cones and the father said, What a perfect day.

John F. Heffernan, firefighter, Ladder 11. His body was found on October 2, his wife's thirty-first birthday.

Michele M. Heidenberger, flight attendant, American Airlines Flight 77. **Sheila M. S. Hein. Howard Joseph Heller. Joann Louise Heltibridle. Petty Officer First Class Ronald J. Hemenway.**

At 9:55 a.m. President Bush boards Air Force One and heads by a circuitous route to Barksdale Air Force Base, outside Shreveport, Louisiana.

Mark F. Hemschoot. September 22 was his twenty-second wedding anniversary.

Ronnie Lee Henderson, firefighter, Engine 279. **Brian Hennessey. Edward R. (Ted) Hennessy Jr. Michelle Marie Henrique. Joseph Patrick Henry,** firefighter, Ladder 21. **William L. Henry Jr.,** firefighter, Rescue 1. **John Christopher Henwood. Robert Allan Hepburn. Mary (Molly) Herencia. Lindsay Coates Herkness III. Harvey Robert Hermer.**

Handyman. Help-desk manager. Hockey scout. Hospice volunteer. Housekeeper. Human resources worker.

Claribel Hernandez. Norberto Hernandez. Sister-in-law and brother-in-law.

Raul Hernandez. Gary Herold. Jeffrey A. Hersch. Thomas Hetzel, firefighter, Ladder 13. **Captain Brian Hickey,** firefighter, Rescue 4; posthumously promoted to battalion chief. **Ysidro Hidalgo-Tejada. Lieutenant Timothy B. Higgins,** firefighter, Special Operations.

On Monday evening she had an argument with her best friend.

Robert D.W. Higley II. Expectant father. His second child, a girl, was born on November 3, 2001.

Todd Russell Hill. Clara Victorine Hinds. Neal O. Hinds. Mark David Hindy. Katsuyuki Hirai. Heather Malia Ho. Tara Yvette Hobbs. Thomas Anderson Hobbs. James L. Hobin. Robert Wayne Hobson. DaJuan Hodges.

Souvenirs. All her life she had saved things. The corsage from her high-school graduation still pinned to the salmon-pink dress she had worn, now three sizes too small. The ticket stubs from a college production of *Hair* that she had attended with a young man she secretly hoped to marry but then he became a draft dodger and moved to Canada and she never saw him again. A lock of her husband's hair from their first date when he took her to a Yankees game. The carbon copies of the airline tickets from their honeymoon trip to Bermuda. All the baby teeth her son had faithfully put under his pillow all those years ago and the Tooth Fairy had never once disappointed him. The umbilical cord stump of her granddaughter who was eight months old now and crawling all over the place, terrifying the cat and getting into everything. (Her son and his wife didn't know she'd kept the stump but she figured what they didn't know wouldn't hurt them.)

Ronald George Hoerner. September 11 was his mother's eighty-fourth birthday. He had been married for eight months.

Patrick Aloysius Hoey. John A. Hofer. Marcia Hoffman. Stephen G. Hoffman.

The end of the day. Any number of things could be relied upon to provide whatever measure of consolation or reward was required at five o'clock (or six or seven or eight). The budget analyst would have a brisk workout at the neighborhood gym. The finance manager would go for a short run with Mozart or Bob Marley on the Walkman. The marketing director would spend an hour in the garden. The tax auditor would have a hot shower and then a cold beer. The flight attendant would have a dry martini with extra olives. Yes, please. Just one.

Frederick Joseph Hoffmann. Michele Lee Hoffmann. Father and daughter.

Judith Florence Hofmiller. She was to be married in October 2001.

Major Wallace Cole Hogan Jr. Thomas Warren Hohlweck Jr. Jonathan R. Hohmann, firefighter, Haz-Mat 1. **Cora Hidalgo Holland. John Holland.**

Vertigo. It had come upon her suddenly about two years ago. The doctor said it was due to a buildup of calcium carbonate crystals within the inner ear. He also said that in half of all cases no cause was ever found. At first she found it alarming because she worked on the 98th floor. But in fact it had nothing to do with height, was just as likely to flare up at home in her ground-floor apartment, when she was bending down to feed the cat or tie her shoes, reaching up to change a lightbulb or sweep a cobweb from the ceiling. Sometimes it happened when she was just walking down the street, minding her own business. It was not dizziness exactly. Rather it was as if the whole world had suddenly come loose from its foundations and was moving in silent waves, undulating around her with no still point upon which she could focus her eyes or her feet.

Joseph Francis Holland. September 11 was his first day back to work from paternity leave. His first child, a boy, was less than two weeks old.

Jimmie Ira Holley. Elizabeth Holmes. Thomas P. Holohan, firefighter, Engine 6. **Herbert Wilson Homer. First Officer LeRoy Wilton Homer Jr.,** copilot, United Airlines Flight 93. **Bradley V. Hoorn.**

In the dream there was an atomic bomb shaped like a bullet, long and silver with a pointed end. Everyone was huddled in the basement. Someone was crying. Another bomb was coming. Its lights were flickering on the radar screen that had appeared on the window of the washing machine. There was a smell of sulfur and burning rubber. There was a whistling sound. The first bomb hit the house but didn't go off. The second bomb was circling the chimney, but then it turned into a paper airplane and floated away. Everyone came up from the basement and sang hymns in the kitchen. Then they had supper and went to bed while it was still light.

James Patrick Hopper. Brother-in-law of **Richard N. Poulos,** also killed.

Montgomery McCullough Hord. Michael J. Horn. Matthew Douglas Horning. Robert L. Horohoe Jr. First Officer Michael Robert Horrocks, copilot, United Airlines Flight 175. **Aaron Horwitz. Charles Joseph Houston.**

Firehouse. They cleaned out their lockers. They got drinks from the soda machine in the hallway. They played cards for money or not. They read cookbooks, spy novels, history books, the poetry of Walt Whitman, the philosophies of Nietzsche, Hegel, and Kant. They studied for departmental exams. They told stories about their fathers, their grandfathers, their uncles, their brothers, who had all been firefighters, too. They passed around photos of their children, their dogs, and their cars. They compared tattoos. They dozed off in front of the television. They called their wives to see how things were going at home.

Uhuru Gonja Houston, police officer, Port Authority. Best friend of **Clinton Davis,** police officer, Port Authority, also killed. Their bodies were found together.

Angela M. Houtz. George Gerald Howard, police officer, Port Authority. **Brady Kay Howell. Michael C. Howell.**

Hope.

Steven Leon Howell. Best friend of **Martin Giovinazzo Jr.,** also killed.

Jennifer L. Howley-Dorsey. She was five months pregnant with her first child.

Milagros (Millie) Hromada. Marian R. Hrycak. Stephen Huczko Jr., police officer, Port Authority.

Horror.

Kris Robert Hughes. Melissa Marie Harrington Hughes. Paul Rexford Hughes. Robert Thomas (Bobby) Hughes. Thomas F. Hughes Jr. Timothy Robert Hughes.

The things they loved. She loved bowling. He loved NASCAR racing. She loved ice skating at Rockefeller Center. He loved hunting deer, ducks, and geese. She loved doing needlepoint. He loved dressing up as the firehouse Santa Claus. She loved rollerblading. He loved moths and always put them back outside safely when they flew into the house. She loved the hummingbirds that came to the kitchen window box. He loved English morris dancing. She loved all things French. He loved walking in the woods. She loved competitive disco dancing. He loved chewing ice. She loved giving people funny nicknames. He loved the Rascals. She loved Faith Hill. He loved Metallica. She loved Roy Orbison. He loved Frank Zappa. She loved John Coltrane. He loved Eric Clapton, The Who, Mountain, and Dave Mason.

Susan Huie. Lamar Demetrius Hulse. John Nicholas Humber Jr. William Christopher Hunt. Kathleen Anne Hunt-Casey. Joseph G. Hunter, firefighter, Squad 288. **Peggie M. Hurt. Robert R. Hussa. Lieutenant Colonel Stephen Neil Hyland Jr. Lieutenant Colonel Robert J. Hymel (retired).**

The things they hated. He hated cursing and swearing of any kind by anyone at any time. She hated telemarketers. He hated getting up early and needed three alarm clocks to wake him. She hated staying up late. He hated doing the laundry. She hated dieting, although she seemed to be doing a lot of it lately. He hated squirrels because they stole the tomatoes from his garden. She hated wearing panty hose. He hated wearing blue jeans. She hated musicals. He hated being late. She hated going to the doctor. He hated getting his hair cut. She hated washing windows. He hated having to wait in line for anything. She hated sweating. He hated parties. She hated meetings. He hated having his picture taken. She hated looking less than her best and would not even go out to buy milk without combing her hair and putting on her lipstick.

Thomas Edward Hynes. Expectant father. His first child, a girl, was born on March 28, 2002.

Captain Walter G. Hynes, firefighter, Ladder 13.

At 9:58 a.m. Lisa Jefferson, a Verizon Airfone emergency supervisor in Chicago, receives a call from Todd Beamer, a passenger on United Airlines Flight 93, declaring that the plane has been hijacked.

I

Joseph Anthony Ianelli Jr. Zuhtu Ibis. Jonathan Lee Ielpi, firefighter, Squad 288.

Illustrator. Import manager. Industrial engineer. Information officer. Information systems technician. Insurance adjuster. Insurance broker. Insurance underwriter. Intelligence officer. Interior decorator. Investment banker. Ironworker.

Michael Patrick Iken. September 8 was his thirty-seventh birthday.

Daniel Ilkanayev. Captain Frederick Ill Jr., firefighter, Ladder 2. **Abraham Nethanel Ilowitz. Anthony P. Infante Jr.,** police inspector, Port Authority. **Louis Steven Inghilterra Jr. Christopher Noble Ingrassia. Paul William Innella. Stephanie Veronica Irby.**

Imagine.

Douglas Jason Irgang. He was to be married on December 22, 2001.

Todd A. Isaac. Erik Hans Isbrandtsen. Taizo Ishikawa. Waleed Joseph Iskandar. Aram Iskenderian Jr.

Impossible.

John F. Iskyan. Lifelong friend of **Thomas Daniel Burke** and **James Lee Connor,** also killed. His sixteenth wedding anniversary was in September.

Kazushige Ito. Aleksandr Valeryerich Ivantsov. Sergeant Major Lacey B. Ivory.

Innocent.

J

Virginia May Jablonski.

At 9:59:04 a.m. Tower 2, the South Tower, collapses. The seismograph station at Palisades, New York, 21 miles north of Lower Manhattan, operated by the Lamont-Doherty Earth Observatory of Columbia University, registers the seismic equivalent of the collapse at 2.1 on the Richter scale for a duration of 10 seconds.

Bryan Creed Jack. On September 11, he had been married for two weeks.

Brooke Alexandra Jackman. Aaron Jeremy Jacobs.

Jumping.

Ariel Louis Jacobs. September 16 was his thirtieth birthday. Expectant father. His first child, a boy, was born on September 17, 2001. September 23 was his first wedding anniversary.

Jason Kyle Jacobs. Michael Grady Jacobs. Steven A. Jacobson. Steven D. (Jake) Jacoby. Ricknauth Jaggernauth. Jake Denis Jagoda. Yudh Vir Singh Jain. Maria Jakubiak. Robert Adrien Jalbert. Ernest James. Gricelda E. Garo James.

On the train every day, two hours each way, she read cookbooks as if they were novels. The story unfolded slowly, the action building chapter by chapter, through Appetizers, Soups, Salads, Side Dishes, and Bread. Entrées were the climax, and desserts, of course, were the delicious denouement. Some were like novels set in foreign countries with exotic locales. In these the characters were mysterious and unpredictable, with names like Machli Ki Tikka, Kruang Kaeng Dang, and Obgusht. Others were like domestic novels set in ordinary middle-class America with familiar friendly characters like pot roast, pork chops, grilled cheese, brownies, and cream of mushroom soup. In these she recognized herself on every page: her kitchen, her stove, her frying pans and spatulas, her hands stirring the batter, her family cleaning their plates and asking for more.

Mark Steven Jardim. Amy N. Jarret, flight attendant, United Airlines Flight 175. **Muhammadou Jawara. François Jean-Pierre. Maxima Jean-Pierre. Paul Edward Jeffers. John Charles Jenkins. Joseph Jenkins Jr. Alan Keith Jensen. Prem Nath Jerath. Farah Jeudy. Hweidar Jian. Eliezer Jiménez Jr. Luis Jiménez Jr.**

Recovered: 144 rings.

Charles Gregory John. Nicholas John. Lieutenant Dennis M. Johnson. Lashawana Johnson. Scott Michael Johnson. William R. Johnston, firefighter, Engine 6.

New York City sports teams. He loved them all: the Yankees, the Mets, the Giants, the Jets, the Rangers, the Islanders, the Liberty, the Knicks, the Metrostars, and the Saints. Whenever it happened that two New York teams were playing against each other, he had to flip a coin to decide which one to root for.

Allison Hortsmann Jones. Arthur Joseph Jones. Brian Leander Jones. Charles Edward Jones. Christopher D. Jones. Donald Thomas Jones II. Donald W. Jones. Judith L. Jones. Linda Joyce Jones. Mary S. Jones.

Quitting time. Having smoked for nineteen years, he had now *not* smoked for three months, two weeks, and five days. He had tried quitting at least a dozen times before, but he had never made it this far. He had tried the patch, the gum, hypnosis, and group therapy. This time he'd gone cold turkey. He was relying strictly on willpower and determination. He had given away all the ashtrays in the house and the Zippo lighter his older brother had given him for Christmas ten years ago. This time he was really going to do it: on his next birthday he would turn forty, and he would be reborn as a nonsmoker.

Andrew B. Jordan, firefighter, Ladder 132. **Robert Thomas Jordan. Albert Gunnia Joseph. Ingeborg Joseph. Karl Henri Joseph,** firefighter, Engine 207. **Stephen Joseph.**

Janitor. Jazz singer. Junior accountant. Junior manager. Junior trader.

Jane Eileen Josiah. Lieutenant Anthony Jovic, firefighter, Battalion 47. **Angel Luis Juarbe Jr.,** firefighter, Ladder 12. **Karen Susan Hawley Juday. Ann Campana Judge. The Reverend Mychal F. Judge,** FDNY chaplain. **Paul William Jurgens,** police officer, Port Authority.

Police. New York's Finest. Bus squad. Bomb squad. Intelligence coordinator. Traffic officer. Sniper. PATH officer. Patrolman. Transit officer. Flag bearer with Port Authority Honor Guard. Holland Tunnel officer. Academy instructor. Lincoln Tunnel officer. Rescue specialist. Court liaison officer in charge of transporting prisoners. Sharpshooter trained in counterterrorism tactics.

Emergency Service Unit: experts in scuba diving, rappelling, marksmanship, first aid, psychology, chemical identification, and the handling of hazardous materials.

Thomas Edward Jurgens. On September 11, he had been married for three months.

K

Shashi Kiran Lakshmikantha Kadaba. Gavharoi Mukhometovna (Gohar) Kamardinova. Shari Ann Kandell.

On Monday night they made love for the first time.

Howard Lee Kane. Jennifer Lynn Kane. Vincent D. Kane, firefighter, Engine 22; posthumously promoted to fire marshal.

At 10:00 a.m. the American military is put on high alert.

Joon Koo Kang. Sheldon Robert Kanter. Deborah H. Kaplan. Robin Lynne Kaplan. Alvin Peter Kappelmann Jr. Charles Henry Karczewski. William Anthony Karnes.

Friday night, Shabbat. The television was turned off, also the computer, the CD player, and the telephone. The children were called to the table. The menorah was lit and blessed. The white tablecloth was laid out and the challah, two loaves of bread, braided and dotted with raisins, was covered with a blue and white cloth and blessed. The wine was poured and blessed. The meal was served and blessed. Later they would sing.

Douglas Gene Karpiloff, director of security and life safety for the World Trade Center. **Charles L. Kasper,** firefighter, deputy chief, Special Operations

Command Battalion; posthumously promoted to battalion chief. **Andrew Keith Kates. John Katsimatides. Sergeant Robert Michael Kaulfers,** police officer, Port Authority. **Don Jerome Kauth Jr. Hideya Kawauchi.**

The streets were choked with yellow cabs, many of the drivers leaning on their horns with energetic exasperation. The sidewalks were crowded with pedestrians, all of them, it seemed, gesturing dramatically and hollering into their cell phones. They surged across intersections in packs whether the light was green, yellow, or red. This caused another outbreak of horn blowing by the cab drivers, many of whom were now also gesturing dramatically and hollering. It was the young man's first visit to Manhattan, and he was thrilled to find that it was exactly the way he had imagined it would be.

Edward Thomas Keane. Richard M. Keane. Lisa Yvonne Kearney-Griffin. Karol Ann Keasler. Barbara A. Keating. Paul Hanlon Keating, firefighter, Ladder 5. **Leon Russell Keene III.**

Secrets. Some people knew. His wife knew, of course, and his children knew. His grandchildren knew. His best friend and his wife knew, but they had been sworn to secrecy, an oath they had so far honored impeccably. Some people must never know, especially the guys at work who were a raucous macho bunch, and if they ever found out, he was sure they would never let him live it down. The guys at work must never know that as a boy he had won several dance competitions and as a young man he had studied ballet. His wife said he was so clumsy that they wouldn't believe it anyway, but he wasn't willing to risk the endless string of tutu jokes such a revelation was bound to elicit.

Brenda Kegler. Best friend of **Carrie R. Blagburn,** also killed.

Chandler Raymond (Chad) Keller. On September 11, he had been married for seven weeks.

Joseph John Keller. Peter Rodney Kellerman. Joseph P. Kellett. Frederick Robert Kelley Jr. James Joseph Kelly.

When the baby took his first steps, he pulled himself up to the coffee table and then staggered over to his mother, who was sitting in the big armchair in the corner. There was much applause and picture taking.

Joseph Anthony Kelly. Expectant father. His fifth child, a boy, was born on May 2, 2002.

Maurice Patrick Kelly. Richard John Kelly Jr., firefighter, Ladder 11. **Thomas Michael Kelly. Thomas Richard Kelly,** firefighter, Ladder 105; posthumously promoted to lieutenant.

At 10:06 a.m. United Airlines Flight 93, traveling at nearly 600 mph, crashes in a field near Shanksville, Pennsylvania, 80 miles southeast of Pittsburgh.

Thomas W. Kelly, firefighter, Ladder 15. September 18 was his fifty-first birthday.

Timothy Colin Kelly. On September 11, his third child, a girl, was eight days old.

William Hill Kelly Jr. Robert Clinton Kennedy.

Falling. When she was six she fell off a swing at the park and broke her left arm. When she was eight she fell off her bicycle and broke her right arm. When she was twelve she fell out of a tree and cracked her collarbone. When she was eighteen she fell down the stairs at a party and broke two ribs. When she was twenty-four she fell off a horse at her cousin's farm and broke her left leg. When she was thirty she fell on the ice in the driveway and suffered a mild concussion. Then, thank God, she went for almost a decade without an accident. Just when she thought she had finally fulfilled her quota of injuries, she slipped in the bathtub and broke her left ankle. So here she was again, hobbling around on crutches and letting people write silly things on her cast.

Thomas J. Kennedy, firefighter, Ladder 101. On September 11, his second child, a boy, was ten months old. On September 14, the baby took his first steps.

John Richard Keohane. Ralph Francis Kershaw. Lieutenant Ronald T. Kerwin, firefighter, Squad 288.

The things they loved. He loved sitting on the back deck with a Coors Light and a cigar. She loved riding horses. He loved singing at parties. She loved going for a Sunday drive. He loved playing tennis. She loved playing volleyball. He loved playing darts. She loved playing miniature golf. He loved playing the electric guitar. She loved playing with her granddaughter's Barbie dolls. He loved playing with his son's Legos. She loved expensive clothes. He loved electric trains. She loved country-western line dancing. He loved the tango. She loved wearing funny socks. He loved wearing bright colors. She loved wearing black, black, and black. He loved making collages. She loved making quilts. He loved doing magic tricks. She loved Martha Stewart. He loved Emeril. She loved letting her parakeet fly around the apartment. He loved talking to the fish in his aquarium. She loved her albino hamster. He loved his dogs, all eight of them.

Howard L. Kestenbaum. Best friend and mentor of **Vijayashankar Paramsothy,** also killed.

Douglas D. Ketcham. Ruth Ellen Ketler. Boris Khalif. Norma Cruz Khan. Sarah Khan. Taimour Firaz Khan.

Kaddish.

Rajesh Khandelwal. Sei-Lai Khoo. Michael Vernon Kiefer, firefighter, Ladder 132. **Satoshi Kikuchihara. Andrew Jay-Hoon Kim. Lawrence Donald Kim. Mary Jo Kimelman. Heinrich Kimmig. Karen Ann Kincaid.**

Kaddish. *Glorified and sanctified be God's great name throughout the world which he has created according to his will. May he establish his kingdom in your lifetime and during your days, and within the life of the entire house of Israel, speedily and soon; and say, Amen.*

May his great name be blessed forever and to all eternity.

Amy R. King, flight attendant, United Airlines Flight 175. Girlfriend of **Michael C. (Mac) Tarrou,** flight attendant, United Airlines Flight 175, also killed.

Andrew Marshall King. Lucille Teresa King. Robert King Jr., firefighter, Engine 33.

Kaddish. *Blessed and praised, glorified and exalted, extolled and honored, adored and lauded be the name of the Holy One, blessed be he, beyond all the blessings and hymns, praises and consolations that are ever spoken in the world; and say, Amen.*

May there be abundant peace from heaven, and life, for us and for all Israel; and say, Amen.

As he has brought peace to heaven, so may he bring peace to us and to Israel; and say, Amen.

Lisa M. King-Johnson. On September 11, she had been married for almost four months.

Brian K. Kinney. Takashi Kinoshita. Chris Michael Kirby. Howard (Barry) Kirschbaum. Glenn Davis Kirwin. Richard Joseph Klares. Peter Anton Klein. Alan David Kleinberg. Karen Joyce Klitzman. Ronald Philip Kloepfer, police officer, NYPD. **Andrew Knox. Thomas Patrick Knox. Yevgeny Knyazev. Rebecca Lee Koborie.**

At 10:10 a.m. a large portion of the Pentagon collapses. Four hundred thousand square feet of floor space are destroyed, and another 2 million square feet are damaged.

Deborah A. Kobus. She became engaged on September 3, 2001.

Gary Edward Koecheler.

Backyard birdwatching. The father sat in the lawn chair with the bird book. His young daughter had the binoculars. He read to her about each bird she spotted. *The blue jay eats sunflower seeds, acorns, fruit, nuts, and insects. The cardinal will fight its own reflection in the window. The downy woodpecker has a barbed tongue and the male sits on the eggs at night. The goldfinch flies up and down like a roller coaster.* Eventually the little girl got so excited that she clapped her hands and scared all the birds away. So they went back into the house and had some lunch.

Frank J. Koestner. He was to be married on October 28, 2001.

Ryan Kohart. Vanessa Lynn Przybylo Kolpak. Irina Kolpakova. Suzanne Kondratenko. Abdoulaye Koné. Bon-seok Koo. Dorota Kopiczko. Scott Kopytko, firefighter, Ladder 15. **Bojan Kostic.**

Keyboard specialist. Kitchen assistant.

Danielle Kousoulis. September 26 was her thirtieth birthday.

David P. Kovalcin. John Joseph Kren. William E. Krukowski, firefighter, Ladder 21. **Lyudmila Ksido. Toshiya Kuge.**

Patriot. *I pledge allegiance to the flag of the United States of America.* For twenty years he had flown the Stars and Stripes in the middle of his front lawn. *And to the Republic for which it stands.* He had a selection of flag T-shirts, baseball caps, and lapel pins. He had three flag bumper stickers, a flag travel mug, a flag bandanna, and a flag tie. He had a car flag. *One nation under God, indivisible.* Every time he heard "God Bless America" or "America the Beautiful" his hand automatically went to his heart. *With liberty and justice for all.* Sometimes a lump formed in his throat and his eyes filled with tears.

Shekhar Kumar. On September 11, he had been married for two months.

Kenneth Kumpel, firefighter, Ladder 25; posthumously promoted to fire marshal. **Frederick Kuo Jr. Patricia Kuras. Nauka Kushitani. Thomas Joseph Kuveikis,** firefighter, Squad 252. **Victor Kwarkye. Kui Fai (Raymond) Kwok. Angela Reed Kyte.**

On Monday evening their mother showed them the old home movies she'd just had transferred to video. They watched their younger selves cavorting in the backyard with a yellow Lab named Sandy who had died twenty years before. They watched Sandy feeding her first litter of six. Their dead father, young again, handsome and muscular, bare chested, washed the new car in the driveway: a 1959 two-tone Ford Fairlane he'd won in a raffle. They watched their parents dancing at their cousin's wedding, their mother in a short red dress with sequins on the bodice, their father in a shiny gray suit and a black bow tie. He toasted the camera with a bottle of beer, winking, grinning, and finally, sticking out his tongue. Then their mother pushed her face in front of his, so close to the camera they could see the smear of lipstick below her bottom lip.

L

Kathryn L. LaBorie, flight attendant, United Airlines Flight 175. **Amarnauth Lachhman. Andrew LaCorte. Ganesh (Shri) Ladkat. James Patrick Ladley. Joseph A. LaFalce. Jeanette Louise LaFond-Menichino. David J. LaForge,** firefighter, Ladder 20.

Lunch hour. Most days she ate a sandwich and a blueberry muffin at her desk and then went down to the bookstore in the northeast plaza. First she browsed the front tables of new releases, and then she scanned the shelves of remainders looking for bargains. She tried, often unsuccessfully, to limit herself to buying only one or two books a week. Even at that, her husband had begun to complain mildly about the number of books that were now overflowing their shelves and ending up in piles in odd places all around the apartment. You already have enough books, he said. To her there was no such thing as enough books. There was only not enough room and not enough money.

Michael Patrick LaForte. September 11 was his thirty-ninth birthday. Expectant father. His third child, a boy, was born on November 14, 2001.

Alan Charles Lafrance. Juan Lafuente. Neil Kwong-Wah Lai. Vincent Anthony Laieta.

Unlucky. Despite buying innumerable lottery tickets, entering hundreds of contests by mail, and traveling twice to Las Vegas, she had never won anything in her life, unless you counted that alarm clock she won at a church bingo when she was twelve and it never worked right anyway. She could never find a parking space anywhere close to where she needed one. She had been divorced twice (both husbands had been unfaithful), and all the nice men she met these days were either married or gay. She had always wanted to have children but had not been able to. She never won at cards or backgammon or miniature golf. If there was a banana peel anywhere in the vicinity, she would be the one to slip on it. She had always thought of herself as an unlucky person, and so far nothing in her life had ever proved her wrong.

William David Lake, firefighter, Rescue 2. On September 10, he celebrated his twentieth anniversary with the FDNY.

Franco Lalama. Chow Kwan Lam. Lieutenant Michael Scott (Scotty) Lamana. Stephen LaMantia. Amy Hope Lamonsoff. Robert T. Lane, firefighter, Engine 55.

Birthday party. The cake, decorated with glossy white icing and a dozen pink candy roses, was just large enough to bear the virtual forest fire of candles, the tremulous inferno of age. Her friends sang the silly song, six middle-aged women in designer suits warbling off-key, and then she blew out every single candle with a mighty dizzying gust of breath. They clamored for her to make a wish and she did. Like a foolish, lonesome teenager, she wished for a man. They demolished the cake with delight, all diets temporarily suspended. When pressed to reveal the nature of her wish, she told them she'd wished for a promotion.

Brendan Mark Lang. Rosanne P. Lang. Nephew and aunt.

Vanessa Lang Langer. She was four months pregnant with her first child.

Mary Louise Langley.

At 10:13 a.m. the United Nations building in New York City is evacuated.

Peter J. Langone, firefighter, Squad 252. **Thomas Michael Langone,** police officer, NYPD. Brothers.

Michele Bernadette Lanza. Ruth Sheila Lapin. Carol Ann LaPlante. Ingeborg Astrid Desirée Lariby. Robin Blair Larkey. Judith Camilla Frankel Larocque. Christopher Randall Larrabee. Hamidou S. Larry.

City boy. He had lived here all his life. He was used to always being surrounded by people, all 8 million of them. He was accustomed to being wedged shoulder to shoulder in Muzak-filled elevators with a dozen well-dressed, perfumed strangers; to hanging from a strap, swaying hip to hip with vacant-eyed strangers in malodorous subway cars. He had long ago perfected a masterful weave-and-dodge technique for navigating the crowds of pedestrian traffic. He was seldom offended by other people's rudeness, impatience, belligerence, bad breath, or body odor. He was used to being able to look into the windows of the apartment directly across from his, no longer titillated by seeing its inhabitant putting on her makeup every morning naked from the waist up. He had lived here all his life, and he couldn't imagine living anywhere else.

Scott A. Larsen, firefighter, Ladder 15. Expectant father. His fourth child, a boy, was born on September 13, 2001.

John Adam Larson.

First grandchild. After all the months of anticipation (and knitting and shopping and helping her son and daughter-in-law prepare the nursery), finally he was here:

her very own grandson. A healthy eight pounds at birth, he had already gained two more. He had his father's strong chin, his mother's small nose, his grandmother's (her!) blue eyes, and a full head of dark hair just like his grandfather had before he went bald. All in one baby, a perfect patchwork of genetics. At first she had worried that becoming a grandmother would make her feel old, but in fact she felt rejuvenated. Whenever she held him, her heart leaped with love. Whenever he cried, she grinned and scooped him up again.

Natalie Janis Lasden. Fiancée of **Donald Americo DiTullio,** also killed.

Gary Edward Lasko.

Legacy.

Nicholas Craig Lassman. Best friend of **Abul K. Chowdhury,** also killed.

Paul Laszczynski, police officer, Port Authority. **Jeffrey G. LaTouche. Charles Augustus Laurencin. Stephen James Lauria. Maria LaVache. Denis Francis Lavelle. Jeannine Mary LaVerde. Anna A. Laverty. Steven Lawn. Robert A. Lawrence Jr. Nathaniel Lawson. David W. Laychak. Olabisi Shadie Layeni-Yee. Eugen Gabriel Lazar.**

What remains. One hundred and thirty military uniforms. One hundred and twenty pairs of sunglasses. One hundred and twelve watercolor paintings. One hundred cashmere sweaters. Ninety-two antique watches. Eighty-three snow globes. Seventy-four lipsticks. Sixty-five pairs of shoes. Sixty-three porcelain eagles. Fifty-seven video games. Forty-six baseball caps. Forty-three tropical fish. Forty handmade fully functioning crossbows. Thirty-two Barbie dolls. Twenty-eight model fire trucks. Twenty-five cats.

James Patrick Leahy, police officer, NYPD. **Lieutenant Joseph Gerard Leavey,** firefighter, Ladder 15. **Neil Joseph Leavy,** firefighter, Engine 217. **Robert George LeBlanc. Leon Lebor. Kenneth Charles Ledee. Alan J. Lederman. Elena F. Ledesma. Alexis Leduc.**

On Monday evening the travel agent went to see a fortune-teller whose predictions were predictably optimistic.

Daniel John Lee. Expectant father. He was flying to California to be with his wife for the birth. His second child, a girl, was born on September 13, 2001.

David Shufee Lee. Expectant father. His first child, a boy, was born on February 18, 2002.

Dong C. Lee. Gary H. Lee. Hyun-joon (Paul) Lee. Juanita Lee. Kathryn Blair Lee. Linda C. Lee. Lorraine Mary Lee. Myung-woo Lee. Richard Yun Choon Lee.

The things they loved. He loved his wife's feet, which were perfectly shaped and always pedicured, the toes precisely straight, the nails polished like pearls, the arches so graceful and tantalizingly ticklish. She loved her husband's hands, which she thought of as healing hands because they were so gentle and warm, and which intrigued her because the lifeline curved halfway up the palm and then stopped. He loved the way his wife cooked chicken, once a week for twenty years now, her own special recipe, slowly baked with gravy and a delectable mixture of rice and vegetables. She had tried to teach him how to make it, but he could never master it. He said she could never leave him because he would starve to death without her chicken dinners.

Soo-Jin (Stuart) Lee. September 12 was his thirty-first birthday.

Yang Der Lee. Stephen Paul Lefkowitz. Adriana Legro. Edward Joseph Lehman. Eric Andrew Lehrfeld. David Ralph Leistman. David Prudencio LeMagne, police officer, Port Authority. **Joseph Anthony Lenihan. John J. (Jay) Lennon Jr.,** police officer, Port Authority. **John Robinson Lenoir. Jorge Luis Leon.**

Recovered: 119 earrings.

Matthew Gerard Leonard. On September 11, his first child, a girl, was seven months old.

Michael Lepore.

Twenty questions. It was a game they had played fifteen years ago, when they first fell in love and still liked to stay up all night talking. What is your favorite color? What is your favorite movie? What was your most embarrassing moment ever? Who was your first love? The questions then were easy and innocent. But now that they were older, it was no longer a game, and the questions were more serious, usually asked now in rare stolen moments of privacy. With five children and two demanding jobs, they were too tired these days to stay up all night talking. Now they asked: What is the worst thing you can think of? If you knew you had only six months to live, what would you do? If you died tomorrow, what would you miss the most? If I died first, would you stay in the house? If I died first, would you remarry?

Charles Antoine Lesperance. He was to be married on November 24, 2001.

Jeffrey Earle LeVeen. John Dennis Levi, police officer, Port Authority. **Alisha Caren Levin. Neil David Levin. Robert Levine. Robert Michael Levine.**

In the center of the coffee table there was a shallow gold-rimmed glass bowl filled with potpourri. Flanking the bowl were two transparent tea-colored pillar candles on frosted glass bases. Their twin flames burned steadily. Their fragrance was elegant and elusive.

Shai Levinhar. On September 11, his first child, a girl, was five and a half weeks old.

Daniel M. Lewin. Adam Jay Lewis.

In the center of the coffee table there was a ramshackle Lego structure that could have been a rocket ship, a skyscraper, or a dinosaur. To the left of the Lego creation was a plastic *Star Wars* plate bearing the remnants of a snack: three broken crackers and a curling slice of orange cheese. To the right was a Batman action figure whose head had fallen off and rolled under the couch.

Kenneth E. Lewis, flight attendant, American Airlines Flight 77. **Jennifer Lewis,** flight attendant, American Airlines Flight 77. Husband and wife.

Margaret Susan Lewis. Ye Wei Liang. Orasri Liangthanasarn. Daniel F. Libretti, firefighter, Rescue 2. **Ralph M. Licciardi. Edward Lichtschein. Samantha Lightbourn-Allen.**

Life, interrupted.

Steven Barry Lillianthal. On September 11, his third child, a boy, was three months old.

Carlos R. Lillo, FDNY paramedic, Battalion 49. **Craig Damian Lilore.**

Bathtime. His wife was in the house all day with their two toddlers and once he got home from work, he took over. After supper he chased them into the bathroom and got them in the tub. Accompanied by an array of rubber ducks, windup boats, and bars of soap shaped like cartoon characters, they giggled and squealed and splashed water all over him. He drew beards and mustaches on them with the bubbles. He washed their hair carefully (no soap in the eyes!) and then scooped them up one at a time in giant fluffy bath towels. He patted them dry, tickled their tummies, and put on their pajamas. It was his favorite time of the day.

Arnold A. Lim. He became engaged at the end of August.

Darya Lin. Wei Rong Lin. Nickie L. Lindo. Thomas V. Linehan Jr. Robert Thomas Linnane, firefighter, Ladder 20. **Alan P. Linton Jr. Diane Theresa Lipari. Kenneth P. Lira. Francisco Alberto Liriano. Lorraine Lisi. Paul Lisson. Vincent M. Litto. Ming-Hao Liu. Nancy Liz.**

Anniversary. Once a year they had dinner at Windows on the World, just the two of them, to celebrate the anniversary not of their wedding but of their engagement. He had proposed to her there twenty-five years ago, when the restaurant had just opened. He had done it the right way, got down on one knee and whispered his prepared speech, clutching the blue velvet ring box in both sweaty hands. He could still remember how relieved he was when she said yes immediately and then burst into tears. Everyone in the restaurant applauded, and he turned bright red, with pride as much as anything. He slipped the ring on her finger and gave a little bow as she hugged him and wept.

Harold Lizcano. On September 11, he had been married for three months.

Martin Lizzul. On September 11, he had been married for three months.

George A. Llanes. September 13 was his thirty-fourth birthday.

Elizabeth Claire (Beth) Logler. She was to be married on December 30, 2001.

Catherine Lisa Loguidice. She was to be married on October 19, 2001.

Jérôme Robert Lohez. Michael William Lomax. Major Stephen Vernon Long. Laura Maria Longing.

At 10:22 a.m. the State Department, the Justice Department, and the World Bank in Washington, D.C., are evacuated.

Salvatore P. Lopes. Daniel Lopez. George Lopez. Luis Manuel Lopez. Maclovio (Joe) Lopez Jr. Manuel L. Lopez.

Lawyer. Legal secretary. Lifeguard. Lobbyist. Locksmith.

Joseph Lostrangio. Chet Dek Louie. Stuart Seid Louis.

Listen.

Joseph Lovero, volunteer and dispatcher for the Jersey City Fire Department. September 8 was his sixtieth birthday.

Sara Elizabeth Low, flight attendant, American Airlines Flight 11. **Michael W. Lowe. Garry W. Lozier. John Peter Lozowsky. Charles Peter Lucania. Edward (Ted) Hobbs Luckett II. Mark Gavin Ludvigsen.**

At least once a week all summer long a small brown bird, usually a sparrow, sometimes a wren, had flown hard against the living room window and fallen dead to the lawn below.

Lee Charles Ludwig. Sean Thomas Lugano. Daniel Lugo. Marie Lukas. William Lum Jr. Michael P. Lunden. Christopher Edmund Lunder. Anthony Luparello. Gary Frederick Lutnick.

The homeless. Every morning the stockbroker made sure the pockets of his suit jacket were filled with change and small bills so he could give something to the panhandlers stationed near the entrance to his office building. Every weekend the corporate secretary volunteered at the homeless shelter, making beds, laundering towels, and serving meals. Every day at lunch the lawyer bought two sandwiches, one for himself and one for the man who slept on the sidewalk grate at the corner. They were both especially fond of chicken salad on whole wheat. Every winter the bond trader knit a dozen scarves and handed them out to the street people she passed on her way to the subway station. She helped them tie the brightly colored scarves around their shivering necks.

Linda Anne Luzzicone. Girlfriend of **Ralph Gerhardt,** also killed.

Alexander Lygin. He was to be married on October 20, 2001.

CeeCee Lyles, flight attendant, United Airlines Flight 93.

Keeping in touch. He called his parents in Arizona every Sunday afternoon at two o'clock: after church, after lunch, before they went off to their game of golf or shuffleboard or darts. She called her mother in Texas every Tuesday night because that was the day her mother had her radiation treatment. She called her sister in

Chicago every night before bed because her sister was going through a nasty divorce and she needed the support. She called her son every day after school to make sure he was home safely and not hanging out somewhere with those awful friends of his. He called his wife from work three times a day just to say, Hello, I love you, how are the kids? She called her husband ten, twelve, fifteen, sometimes twenty times a day whenever she had to work a flight to the West Coast.

Farrell Peter Lynch. Sean P. Lynch. Brothers. Sean was an expectant father. His third child, a boy, was born on November 12, 2001.

James Francis Lynch, police officer, Port Authority. **James T. Lynch Jr. Louise A. Lynch.**

Loneliness.

Michael F. Lynch, firefighter, Engine 40. He was to be married on November 16, 2001.

Michael Francis Lynch, firefighter, Ladder 4; posthumously promoted to lieutenant. On September 11, his second child, a boy, was seven months old.

Michael (Morty) Lynch. Richard Dennis Lynch Jr. Robert H. Lynch Jr. Sean Patrick Lynch. Terence M. (Terry) Lynch.

Lost.

Michael J. Lyons, firefighter, Squad 41. Expectant father. His second child, a girl, was born on November 2, 2001.

Monica Anne Lyons. Petty Officer Second Class Nehamon Lyons IV.

The new house. In another week the painting would be finished and finally they would be able to move in. The boxes were packed and labeled and stacked in every room of the old apartment. The truck was rented. The new telephone was hooked up and the old one was scheduled to be disconnected. At last, said the husband. At long last, said the wife. The baby gurgled in agreement.

Patrick Lyons, firefighter, Squad 252; posthumously promoted to lieutenant. Expectant father. His first child, a boy, was born on October 7, 2001.

M

Robert Francis Mace. Marianne MacFarlane. Jan Maciejewski. Susan A. MacKay. Catherine Fairfax MacRea. Richard Blaine Madden. Simon Maddison.

The past. Forty-four years ago, when she was five years old, her family was expelled from Cuba and fled to America in a small boat. Forty years ago, as a navy test pilot, he walked away from five separate crash landings. Thirty-six years ago, in Vietnam, he led a platoon through the valley of Ia Drang, where more than two hundred American soldiers died. Thirty-three years ago his mother died while giving birth to him. Thirty-two years ago one of her six children was killed in Vietnam. Thirty years ago, as a young air force pilot, his B-52 was shot down by a North Vietnamese surface-to-air missile. Thirty years ago, in Vietnam, he lost a leg in combat and then spent several days alone in the jungle.

Noell C. Maerz. Expectant father. His first child, a girl, was born on October 31, 2001.

Jeannieann Maffeo. Joseph Maffeo, firefighter, Ladder 101. **Jay Robert Magazine. Brian Magee. Charles Wilson Magee. Joseph V. Maggitti. Ronald E. Magnuson. Daniel L. Maher.**

The future. She dreamed of opening her own real estate firm. He dreamed of retiring early and moving to Key West. She dreamed of owning a soul food restaurant. He dreamed of returning to his homeland and building a house. She dreamed of opening a candy store. He dreamed of writing and illustrating children's books. She dreamed of publishing a book of poetry. He dreamed of becoming a navy pilot. She dreamed of becoming a criminal lawyer. He dreamed of becoming an actor. She dreamed of becoming an opera singer. He dreamed of becoming a rock star.

Thomas Anthony Mahon. William J. Mahoney II, firefighter, Rescue 4. **Joseph Daniel Maio. Takashi Makimoto. Abdu Ali Malahi. Debora I. Maldonado.**

Identical twins. He could not imagine what it was like for other people. People who did not have another half with the same brown eyes flecked with gold, the same unruly hair falling across the forehead, the same full lips curling into the same lopsided smirk, the same bony knees, the same knobby toes with the second toe longer than the rest. He could not imagine what it was like not to have a mirror image of yourself that talked the same, laughed the same, thought the same, probably kissed the same, and occasionally dressed the same, at one time because their mother thought it was cute and now because, shopping separately in different stores, they often bought the very same shirts, shoes, and underwear. He could not imagine what it was like to be alone in the world.

Myrna T. Maldonado-Agosto. On September 11, she had been married for five months to a man she had first met forty years ago.

Alfred Russell Maler. Gregory James Malone.

At 10:24 a.m. all international flights bound for American destinations are diverted to Canada. Two hundred and forty planes are landed in Halifax,

Moncton, St. John's, Calgary, Edmonton, Vancouver, Toronto, and other Canadian cities. The small town of Gander, Newfoundland, population 10,000, takes in 10,500 passengers from more than fifty planes.

Edward Francis (Teddy) Maloney III. Expectant father. His second child, a girl, was born on December 4, 2001.

Joseph E. Maloney, firefighter, Ladder 3. **Gene Edward Maloy. Christian Hartwell Maltby.**

Former lives. Nobody's life turned out exactly the way they had hoped, expected, assumed, or imagined it would. Of course she knew that. Everybody knew that. And yet she was still surprised to find herself here: a small-town prom queen from the heartland living now in a shabby apartment in a questionable neighborhood in a city of more than 8 million people, working two jobs just to make ends meet and still there was never enough money, raising four teenagers on her own and hardly a day went by without a crisis of some sort. She was afraid to think too hard about the future, and how on earth had all this happened to her of all people?

Francisco Miguel (Frank) Mancini. On September 11, his first child, a girl, was three months old.

Joseph Mangano. Debra M. Mannetta. Marion Victoria (Vickie) Manning. Terence John Manning. James Maounis. Alfred Gilles Padre Joseph Marchand, flight attendant, United Airlines Flight 175. **Joseph Ross Marchbanks Jr.,** firefighter, deputy chief, Battalion 57; posthumously promoted to battalion chief. **Laura A. Marchese-Giglio. Hilda Marcin.**

Maelstrom.

Peter Edward Mardikian. On September 11, he had been married for six weeks.

Edward Joseph Mardovich. September 10 was his sixteenth wedding anniversary.

Lieutenant Charles Joseph (Chuck) Margiotta, firefighter, Battalion 22. **Louis Neil Mariani.**

Mysteries. The receptionist read two or three every week, so many that the characters and their crimes often ran together in her mind. By the end of any given month, she could not remember which woman had murdered her philandering husband by suffocation and which by rat poison. She was no longer sure which man had been arrested for embezzlement and which for sexual harassment. She got mixed up about weapons and motives, alibis and perjuries, evidence and sentences. But she supposed it didn't really matter anyway because in mysteries everything always worked out in the end, and that was why she read them.

Kenneth Joseph Marino, firefighter, Rescue 1. **Lester Vincent Marino. Vita M. Marino.**

Recovered: 80 bracelets.

Kevin D. Marlo. José J. Marrero. John Daniel Marshall, firefighter, Ladder 27. **Shelley A. Marshall. James Martello. Michael A. Marti.**

In the photo album. A street grate in Paris. A license plate in the Virgin Islands. A gondola in Venice. A wrought-iron gate in Barcelona. A stained-glass window in Rome. A windmill in the Netherlands. A historic battlefield in Germany. A statue of a naked woman, armless, in Milan.

Karen Ann Martin, flight attendant, American Airlines Flight 11. **Lieutenant Peter C. Martin,** firefighter, Rescue 2. **Teresa M. Martin. William J. Martin Jr. Brian E. Martineau. Betsy Martinez.**

Birthday party. Next weekend their son would turn six. Eight of his friends were coming over, and the party was all planned. They had hired a clown for Saturday afternoon and ordered a gigantic bunch of helium-filled balloons and a cake in the shape of a yellow dump truck to be picked up that morning. Before the cake, which would, of course, be served with ice cream, they would cook hamburgers and hot dogs on the barbecue. There would also be a large bowl of potato salad that none of the children would eat. They would play some games in the backyard, and then the boy would open his presents. At four o'clock his friends would go home again, happy with their loot bags, all revved up and a little sick to their stomachs after too much excitement and too much sugar. The house would be a mess, the parents would be exhausted, and a good time would have been had by all.

Edward J. Martinez. September 19 was his twentieth wedding anniversary.

José Angel Martinez Jr. Robert Gabriel Martinez. Waleska Martinez. Lizie D. Martínez-Calderón.

In the dream an airplane crashed. Pieces of the plane and human body parts fell from the sky. For ten years the young woman's father had had this recurring dream every few months. Sometimes there were also scorched trees in the dream and men in white suits poking at the burning skeleton of the airplane.

Lieutenant Paul Richard Martini, firefighter, Engine 201. **Joseph A. Mascali,** firefighter, Tactical Support 2. **Bernard Mascarenhas. Stephen Frank Masi. Ada L. Mason-Acker. Nicholas George Massa.**

Mercy.

Patricia Ann Cimaroli Massari. Early on the morning of September 11, she found out she was pregnant with her first child.

Michael Massaroli. On September 11, his second child, a girl, was two months old.

Philip William Mastrandrea Jr. Rudolph Mastrocinque. Joseph Mathai. Charles William Mathers. William A. Matheson. Marcello Matricciano. Margaret Elaine Mattic. Lieutenant Colonel Dean E. Mattson. Robert D. Mattson. Walter Matuza Jr.

The sound of rain on the window in the middle of the night was so soothing and hypnotic, inducing such a deep sleep that when the alarm clock went off in the morning it was as if no time had passed at all.

Lieutenant General Timothy L. Maude. The army's deputy chief of staff for personnel, General Maude was the highest-ranking military officer killed on September 11.

Charles A. (Chuck) Mauro Jr. Charles J. Mauro. Dorothy Mauro. Nancy T. Mauro.

The end of August. It had been the best summer of her life. She had had a great vacation in California with her best friend. She had learned how to sail. She had found the perfect job, which she would begin early in September. She had lost ten pounds and got her hair cut short. She had found a terrific apartment that she could actually afford. She had signed up for aerobics. And best of all, she had met

a wonderful man who could just be *the one.* All in all, she wrote in an e-mail to her sister, she was so happy she could hardly stand it.

Robert J. Maxwell. Renée Ann May, flight attendant, American Airlines Flight 77. **Tyrone May. Keithroy Marcellus Maynard,** firefighter, Engine 33. **Robert J. Mayo.**

Music. All his life he'd had a gift for musical instruments. He was already skilled at the piano, the guitar, the clarinet, the dulcimer, and the accordion. Now he was learning to play the bagpipes, much to his wife's chagrin. Supportive though she had been of all his previous musical adventures, this time she absolutely could not stand the noise. She said it sounded like he was squeezing a cat under his arm. Bagpipes in a parade were fine, she said, but bagpipes in the house were a different thing altogether. She made him practice in the garage.

Captain Kathy Nancy Mazza-Delosh, police officer, Port Authority. She was the first female commanding officer of its police academy.

Edward J. Mazzella Jr. He was to retire on September 14, 2001.

Jennifer Lynn Mazzotta. Kaaria W. Mbaya. James Joseph McAlary Jr.

Solitude. The woman who lived alone loved coming home each day to her empty apartment: it was so quiet and so clean. She liked to think she had a talent for solitude. She enjoyed her own company and was seldom lonely or bored. She loved being able to come and go as she pleased with no one to ask where she was going and when she would be back, no one to complain when she was late, no one to require an explanation when she changed her plans at the last minute, no one to wait up for her, always worrying and wondering where she could be. She took

an admittedly odd pleasure in imagining that she could be gone for days and no one would notice.

Brian G. McAleese, firefighter, Engine 226. On September 11, his fourth child, a boy, was four months old.

Patricia Ann McAneney. Colin Richard McArthur.

Distinguishing features: tattoos. Unicorn above her left breast. Rescue 2 symbol on his right forearm. Circle of thorns around her right ankle. Heart broken into two jagged pieces on his chest. Yin-yang symbol on his left shoulder. Crescent moon and three stars on the back of her neck. Clover inside horseshoe and shark with anchor inscribed *USN* on left arm, pirate ship on right. Harley-Davidson eagle on his upper right arm, coiled snake with fangs on his right forearm, skull and crossbones on his left forearm, large spider with web on his upper left arm.

John Kevin McAvoy, firefighter, Ladder 3. September 17 was his forty-eighth birthday.

Kenneth M. McBrayer. Brendan F. McCabe. Michael Justin McCabe. Thomas J. McCann, firefighter, Battalion 8.

In the photo album. A chandelier in Grand Central Station. A street sign in Greenwich Village. A fried chicken restaurant in Harlem. The limestone edifice of Temple Emanu-El. The brass door of the Home Savings Bank. The cast-iron facades of Greene Street. A bell in a church in Brooklyn. A fire hydrant spewing water at an intersection in the Bronx. A naked mannequin, armless, in a store window in Soho.

Justin J. McCarthy. September 19 was his thirtieth birthday.

Kevin M. McCarthy. Michael Desmond McCarthy.

A decision. They had been married for three years. Before that they had lived together for two and before that they had dated for five. So they had been together for a total of ten years. They figured it was safe now to say that their relationship would last (despite what anyone might have predicted back at the beginning). They both had good jobs, they were financially secure, they had recently bought an SUV and a three-bedroom house in a good neighborhood. They shared the same views on politics, religion, money, and morals. They thought of themselves as mature, responsible people. If they weren't ready now, they never would be: they decided that in October they would start trying to get pregnant.

Robert Garvin McCarthy. Brother-in-law of **Gerald Thomas O'Leary,** also killed. On September 11, his first child, a boy, was two weeks old.

Stanley McCaskill. Katie Marie McCloskey. Tara McCloud-Gray.

The sound of rain on the window in the middle of the night was depressing and annoying, as bad as a dripping faucet, rendering sleep a fitful and largely futile exercise, turning the night into an endless stretch of waiting for the alarm clock to ring.

Ruth Magdaline Clifford McCourt. Juliana Valentine McCourt. Mother and daughter. Ruth was the best friend of **Paige Marie Farley-Hackel,** also killed.

Charles Austin McCrann. Tonyell F. McDay.

On the fridge door. A recent painting of red, blue, and yellow blobs with black, green, and pink smears, and the boy said it was a picture of the day they went to the museum and saw the dinosaur bones. An old Christmas card featuring two pudgy polar-bear cubs rolling in the snow. A postcard from Canada featuring a castlelike hotel with a green roof against a deep blue sky and thousands of orange and yellow tulips all around it. A photograph of the boy in a purple jacket in a barnyard petting the nose of a black lamb. An invitation to a birthday party next Saturday with Spiderman smiling on the front. A field-trip permission slip that should have been signed and returned a week ago. A math test with a big gold star at the top. A hand-lettered saying in gold ink on black paper: *Live while you're alive.*

Matthew T. McDermott. Expectant father. His third child, a boy, was born on March 22, 2002.

Joseph P. McDonald. Brian Grady McDonnell, police officer, NYPD. **Michael Patrick McDonnell. John Francis McDowell Jr. Eamon J. McEneaney. John Thomas McErlean Jr. Daniel Francis McGinley. Mark Ryan McGinly. Lieutenant William E. McGinn,** firefighter, Squad 18; posthumously promoted to captain. **Thomas Henry McGinnis. Michael Gregory McGinty.**

At 10:28:31 a.m. Tower 1, the North Tower, collapses. The seismograph station at Palisades, New York, 21 miles north of Lower Manhattan, operated by the Lamont-Doherty Earth Observatory of Columbia University, registers the seismic equivalent of the collapse at 2.3 on the Richter scale for a duration of 8 seconds.

Ann McGovern. Scott Martin McGovern. William J. McGovern, firefighter, chief, Battalion 2.

The World Trade Center complex comprised 7 buildings located on a 16-acre site in Lower Manhattan bounded by Church, West, Liberty, and Vesey streets. Each of the World Trade Center towers was 110 stories high, built on a foundation extending 70 feet below ground. Visible from a distance of 20 miles, they were the world's fifth and sixth tallest buildings. The South Tower was 1,362 feet tall. The North Tower was 1,368 feet tall. Their combined weight was 1.5 million tons. The entire complex contained 12 million square feet of office space with 16 miles of staircases and a daily electricity bill of $3 million.

Stacey Sennas McGowan. Francis Noel McGuinn. First Officer Thomas F. McGuinness Jr., copilot, American Airlines Flight 11. **Patrick J. McGuire.**

Each of the World Trade Center towers contained 104 passenger elevators and 21,800 windows. Together the towers contained 600,000 square feet of glass, 6 acres of marble, 1,200 restrooms, and 828 emergency exit doors. Each floor was a full acre in area. Approximately 50,000 people worked in the World Trade Center, which housed more than 430 companies from nearly 30 different countries. There were 75 stores on the concourse level. Constructed by 10,000 workers between 1966 and 1973, it took 6 years and 8 months to build the Twin Towers. It took 1 hour and 42 minutes to destroy them.

Thomas Michael McHale. Expectant father. His first child, a boy, was born on October 18, 2001.

Keith D. McHeffey. Ann Marie McHugh. Denis J. McHugh III. Dennis P. McHugh, firefighter, Ladder 13. **Michael Edward McHugh Jr. Robert G. McIlvaine.**

Windows on the World occupied the 106th and 107th floors of the North Tower. With annual revenues of $37 million, it was the country's top-grossing restaurant. First opened in 1976, it was damaged in the 1993 bombing and remained closed for three years. Renovated at a cost of $25 million, it was reopened in 1996, a two-acre space with seating for nearly 3,000 people. Windows on the World employed more than 450 people from more than two dozen different countries. On September 11, all 79 employees at work that morning were killed.

Donald James McIntyre, police officer, Port Authority. Brother-in-law of **John Anthony Sherry,** also killed. Expectant father. His third child, a girl, was born on November 27, 2001.

Stephanie Marie McKenna. Molly Hornberger McKenzie. Barry J. McKeon. Evelyn C. McKinnedy.

The international brokerage firm of Cantor Fitzgerald occupied floors 101, 103, 104, and 105 of the North Tower. The firm handled $200 billion of securities a day, or $50 trillion a year. The company employed more than a thousand people in its World Trade Center offices. On September 11, Cantor Fitzgerald lost 658 of those employees, more than any other company. Thirty-eight of the victims' wives were pregnant, fourteen of them for the first time. Forty-six of those killed were engaged to be married, with at least two weddings to take place the following weekend. Nearly twenty sets of siblings were killed in the attack. Nine hundred and fifty-five children lost a parent who worked for Cantor Fitzgerald.

Darryl Leron McKinney. Fiancé of **Angela Rosario,** also killed.

George Patrick McLaughlin Jr. Robert Carroll McLaughlin Jr. Gavin McMahon.

At 10:30 a.m. New York governor George Pataki declares a state of emergency.

Robert Dismas McMahon, firefighter, Ladder 20. Expectant father. His second child, a boy, was born on January 6, 2002.

Edmund M. McNally. Daniel Walker McNeal. Walter Arthur McNeil, police officer, Port Authority. **Christine Sheila McNulty. Sean Peter McNulty. Robert William McPadden,** firefighter, Engine 23. **Terence A. McShane,** firefighter, Ladder 101. **Timothy Patrick McSweeney,** firefighter, Ladder 3.

The things they loved. She loved shoes. He loved trees. She loved sailing. He loved football. She loved white-water rafting. He loved wearing a tuxedo. She loved backpacking. He loved playing practical jokes. She loved playing hide-and-seek. He loved playing charades. She loved playing checkers. He loved ironing. She loved knitting sweaters for her family and friends. He loved milk and drank a gallon of it every day. She loved Banana Republic. He loved Starbucks. She loved Bloomingdale's. He loved the army and navy surplus store. She loved Target. He loved Saks Fifth Avenue. She loved kung fu. He loved St. Patrick's Day, especially the green beer. She loved bouncing on the trampoline in the backyard. He loved making maps. She loved telling jokes. He loved shooting hoops in the driveway with his sons. She loved parades. He loved bungee jumping. She loved Michael Jackson. He loved Aretha Franklin. She loved Fleetwood Mac. He loved old English ballads.

Martin Edward McWilliams, firefighter, Engine 22. On September 11, his first child, a girl, was four months old.

Rocco A. Medaglia. Abigail Cales Medina. Ana Iris Medina. Deborah Louise Medwig.

Monstrous.

Damian Meehan. Expectant father. His second child, a girl, was born on January 24, 2002.

William J. Meehan Jr. Alok Kumar Mehta. Raymond Meisenheimer, firefighter, Rescue 3. **Manuel Emilio Mejía. Eskedar Melaku.**

Mail carrier. Mailroom clerk. Maintenance worker. Management analyst. Management intern for chief of naval intelligence. Managing director. Margins clerk. Marketing director. Mason. Master mechanic. Mechanical engineer. Mediator. Merchant marine. Messenger. Microfiche clerk. Millworker. Minister. Model. Motivational speaker. Museum volunteer. Musician.

Antonio Melendez. Best friend of **Leobardo Lopez Pascual,** also killed.

Mary Melendez. September 27 was her twenty-sixth wedding anniversary.

Christopher D. Mello. Yelena Melnichenko. Stuart Todd Meltzer. Diarelia Jovannah Mena. Dora Marie Menchaca. Charles R. Mendez, firefighter, Ladder 7. **Lizette Mendoza. Shevonne Olicia Mentis. Wolfgang Peter Menzel.**

Secrets. During his twenty-year career as a firefighter, he had received numerous citations for valor, including one for the 1993 bombing of the World Trade Center. He was a modest man, and he seldom talked about his work at home. So he had not mentioned any of these honors to his wife. After all, he had just been doing his job.

Steve Mercado, firefighter, Engine 40. **Wesley Mercer. Ralph Joseph Mercurio. Alan Harvey Merdinger. George Merino. Yamel Merino,** emergency medical technician. **George Merkouris. Deborah A. Merrick. Raymond Joseph Metz III. Jill Ann Metzler. David Robert Meyer.**

On Monday evening they went to their weekly salsa dancing class.

Nurul Huq Miah. Shakila Yasmin Miah. Husband and wife.

William Edward Micciulli. Martin Paul Michelstein. Patricia E. Mickley.

Naming the baby. *Amelia. Andrea. Angus.* All summer they'd been reading the baby-name book in bed at night. *Daniel. Destiny. Devon.* It was too hot to sleep anyway. *Hannah. Iris. Jacob.* Each night they added more names to their list of possibilities. *Madeleine. Matthew. Murray.* Each morning they crossed some of them off again. *Tamara. Travis. Trinity.* Sometimes they disagreed vigorously. *Lester.* Absolutely not, she said. *Carlotta.* Are you crazy, he said. *Boris.* Over my dead body, she said, and threw a pillow at his head.

Major Ronald D. Milam. Expectant father. His second child, a boy, was born on January 6, 2002.

Peter Teague Milano. Gregory Milanowycz.

Last seen wearing. Black pants, shoes, belt; beige shirt with double pockets, silk or rayon; no tie. Black pants, Ralph Lauren shirt and boxers, Hermès tie. Blue long-sleeved shirt, burgundy slacks, orange and white Reeboks. Pullover red shirt with blue stripes, blue pants and socks, black shoes. Baseball cap with Madonna's

Drowned World tour logo. Blue dress pants with no pockets, black and brown shirt, black sandals. Navy blue pants, short-sleeved medium-blue top, tight knee-high orthopedic socks. Brand-new Air Jordan basketball shoes. May have been wearing a black business suit with mid-length skirt, Jigsaw brand. May have been wearing a lime-green blouse.

Lukasz Tomasz Milewski. On July 11, 2001, he arrived in the United States for the first time, having emigrated from Poland.

Sharon Christina Millan. Corey Peter Miller. Craig James Miller. Douglas Charles Miller Jr., firefighter, Rescue 5. **Henry Alfred Miller Jr.,** firefighter, Ladder 105. **Joel Miller.**

Packing. The suitcase was open on the bed. It was filling up with socks, underwear, shirts, pants, shaving kit, an extra pair of shoes, a warm sweater in case the weather turned, small gifts for the nieces and nephews, a swimsuit because the parents had a pool, ten CDs because the parents did not have an appreciation for rap music. The blue plastic pet carrier sat on the floor beside the bed. The dog hated traveling and had to be tranquilized before being put on the plane. He was a smart dog, and as soon as the suitcase and the carrier were taken out of the closet, he knew what was coming. At the moment he was hiding in the basement, hoping to become invisible.

Michael Matthew Miller. He was to be married in October 2001.

Nicole Carol Miller. Phillip D. Miller. Robert Alan Miller. Robert Cromwell Miller Jr.

Lunch hour. Most days he had a sandwich and a coffee at the deli downstairs. If the weather was good, he went for a brisk walk to get some exercise and clear his head. If the weather was bad, he went to the Winter Garden. After all these years he still loved the soaring glass-and-steel architecture of the atrium, the sweeping marble staircase, and the lively piazza. Sometimes he took in a lunch-hour concert or an art show. Sometimes he enjoyed just strolling around and watching the ever-changing crowd. Sometimes it was enough simply to sit and admire the forty-five-foot palm trees that had been transplanted from the Mojave Desert to create this oasis under glass here in the shadow of the Twin Towers.

Benjamin Millman. Charles Morris Mills Jr. Ronald Keith Milstein. Robert Minara, firefighter, Ladder 25. **William George Minardi.**

Gadgets. It had all started with the backup beeper and remote-control starter for the minivan. Then he bought a machine that produced the soothing sounds of white noise, ocean surf, summer night, gentle rain, tumbling waterfall, and mother's heartbeat. Before you knew it, he also owned an electronic mosquito trap, a wireless weather center, a solar-powered lantern with AM/FM radio, a contact-lens-washing machine, an automatic pet dish that would feed the dog up to six meals of both wet and dry food while they were out, and a fingerprint scanner that had not yet proved useful, but he was sure it would come in handy someday. Much as his wife liked to tease him about all his silly gadgets, this year for his birthday she was going to buy him an electric double-buffer shoe polisher and a rechargeable electronic corkscrew.

Louis Joseph Minervino. September 20 was his twenty-sixth wedding anniversary.

Thomas Mingione, firefighter, Ladder 132. Expectant father. His first child, a girl, was born on December 13, 2001.

Wilbert Miraille. Domenick N. Mircovich. Rajesh Arjan Mirpuri. Joseph D. Mistrulli. Susan J. Miszkowicz. Lieutenant Paul Thomas Mitchell, firefighter, Battalion 1. **Richard P. Miuccio.**

When the baby in the high chair at the kitchen table put a full bowl of spaghetti on her head, the mother shrieked and ran for the dishcloth. The sauce and the pasta oozed down the baby's forehead. One small meatball stuck to the tip of her nose. She clapped her hands and hollered happily. The father snorted and laughed and ran for the camera.

Jeffrey Peter Mladenik. He and his wife were in the process of adopting a baby girl from China.

Frank V. Moccia Sr. Captain Louis Joseph Modafferi, firefighter, Rescue 5; posthumously promoted to battalion chief. **Boyie Mohammed. Lieutenant Dennis Mojica,** firefighter, Rescue 1. **Manuel Mojica Jr.,** firefighter, Squad 18.

The Maltese Cross, the firefighter's badge of honor. Originally used in the eleventh century by the Knights of Saint John of Jerusalem, now recognized as the first organized group of firefighters and paramedics. Enlisted to fight against the Saracens during the Crusades to help free the Holy Land, the Knights of Saint John wore the cross as identification on their armor. It came to symbolize the principles of charity, loyalty, sympathy, gallantry, generosity, perseverance, and protection of the weak.

Kleber Rolando Molina. Manuel DeJesus Molina.

The things they carried. Black briefcase containing Apple laptop computer, travel brochures for Italy and France, *Golf Digest,* three chocolate bars. Swiss army knife in pants pocket. Cosmetic bag containing makeup, toothbrush and toothpaste, dental floss, Chanel No. 5 cologne, nasal spray, prescription medications for acid reflux and anxiety. Brown leather purse containing cigarettes in a silver case, an unfinished letter to her mother, a Mont Blanc fountain pen, a tiny can of pepper spray. Russian-English dictionary in jacket pocket. White vinyl purse containing grocery coupons, a crossword puzzle book, a subway map, a hairnet. Small beaded American flag change purse.

Carl E. Molinaro, firefighter, Ladder 2. On September 11, his second child, a boy, was twenty-three days old. Originally named Thomas, the baby's name was changed to Carl after the tragedy.

Justin J. Molisani Jr. Brian Patrick Monaghan Jr. Franklyn Monahan. John Gerard Monahan. Kristen Montanaro. Craig D. Montano. Michael G. Montesi, firefighter, Rescue 1.

In training. This year the New York City Marathon would be run on November 4 and he would be there, one of 30,000 runners, cheered on by his wife, one of 2.5 million spectators lining the 26.2-mile route through the five boroughs of the city. He was already working hard to get ready, determined to better his time of 3 hours and 15 minutes last year. He figured that come November he would be in better shape than he'd ever been in his life.

Carlos Alberto Montoya. Antonio Jesus Montoya-Valdez. Cheryl Ann Monyak. Captain Thomas Moody, firefighter, Division 1. **Sharon Moore-Mohammed. Krishna V. Moorthy. Laura Lee Morabito.**

Public works of art completely or partially destroyed. Fritz Koenig: *Sphere for Plaza Fountain,* 1969; bronze on black granite base; 25 feet high, weighing 22.5 tons; intended to symbolize world peace through world trade. Alexander Calder:

World Trade Center Stabile (also known as *Bent Propeller* and *Three Wings*), 1971; red stainless steel; 25 feet high, weighing 15 tons. Masayuki Nagare: *World Trade Center Plaza Sculpture* (also known as *Cloud Fortress*), 1972; black Swedish granite over steel and concrete armature; 14 feet high, 34 feet wide, 17 feet deep.

Abner Morales. Carlos Manuel Morales. Martín Morales. Paula E. Morales.

Public works of art completely or partially destroyed. Joan Miró: *World Trade Center Tapestry,* 1974; multicolored wool and hemp; 20 feet high, 35 feet wide; located in the lobby of Tower 2. James Rosati: *Ideogram,* 1974; stainless steel; 28 feet high, 23 feet wide. Louise Nevelson: *Sky Gate, New York,* 1977–78; black painted wood relief; made up of more than thirty-five sculptures; located on the mezzanine of Tower 1. Elyn Zimmerman: *World Trade Center Memorial,* 1993; round red, black, and white granite fountain created in honor of the victims of the 1993 bombing; located in front of the Marriott Hotel. The combined value of these seven works of art was between $8 million and $10 million.

Gerard P. (Jerry) Moran Jr. John Moran, firefighter, chief, Battalion 49. **John Christopher Moran. Kathleen Moran.**

At 10:41 a.m. President Bush is aboard Air Force One headed toward Jacksonville, Florida. By telephone, Vice President Dick Cheney advises him not to return immediately to Washington.

Lindsay Stapleton Morehouse. George William Morell. Steven P. Morello. Vincent S. Morello, firefighter, Ladder 35. **Yvette Nicole Moreno. Dorothy Morgan. Richard J. Morgan. Nancy Morgenstern. Sanae Mori.**

A business trip. It was an old and elegant hotel, recently renovated, so close to Lincoln Center, the guidebook said, that you could almost hear the arias. The grand lobby was decorated to resemble a Tudor castle. The young woman saw a famous person when she was checking in, someone from a now canceled television show and she could not quite think of his name. The room was small but, as the guidebook promised, it was stylish and comfortable, equipped with a television, a VCR, a tape deck, and a CD player. It overlooked a small park with wrought-iron benches and a statue of some historical figure she could not identify in the darkness. She unpacked, undressed, and fell asleep quickly despite the sound of traffic, not arias, in the street below. She had an early-morning meeting at the World Trade Center.

Blanca Robertino Morocho. Leonel Geronimo Morocho. Sister and brother. On September 11, Blanca's first child, a girl, was eight months old. Leonel was the father of five children. His three youngest daughters lived with him and his wife in Brooklyn. His two older daughters remained in Ecuador, awaiting the legal papers that would allow them to join the rest of the family. On September 19, they arrived in New York on a humanitarian visa.

Dennis Gerard Moroney. Lynne Irene Morris.

A business trip. In her hotel room the young woman awoke slowly to a persistent and annoying sound from outside. The drapes were so heavy that the room was still dark and she thought it was the middle of the night. Pulling back the drapes, she discovered it was morning, bright and sunny. There were half a dozen joggers circling the little park. Directly below her window, the uniformed hotel doorman stood out in the street, blowing on a large silver whistle and waving his arms at the taxis sailing past. A group of well-dressed people with suitcases huddled on the sidewalk, squinting hopefully at every taxi that came toward them, then turning their heads as one to gaze sadly after each set of receding taillights. She laughed and got dressed. She had an early-morning meeting at the World Trade Center.

Odessa V. Morris. September 11 was her twenty-fifth wedding anniversary.

Seth Allan Morris. Stephen Philip Morris. Christopher Martel Morrison.

Recovered: 77 necklaces.

Jorge Luis Morron. He was to become an American citizen on September 17. Expectant father. His first child was due in March 2002, but the baby was lost on October 4, 2001.

Ferdinand V. (Fred) Morrone, police superintendent, Port Authority. **William David Moskal. Petty Officer Second Class Brian Anthony Moss. Marco (Mark) Motroni Sr. Cynthia Motus-Wilson. Iouri A. Mouchinski. Jude Joseph Moussa. Peter C. Moutos. Damion O'Neil Mowatt.**

The past. Twenty-nine years ago his brother was killed in Vietnam. Twenty-six years ago, when Communists took over South Vietnam, his father and two of his siblings escaped to the United States, but he and his mother and the other children were left behind. Twenty-five years ago, when he was thirteen, his father was murdered. Twenty-two years ago her husband and her brother were killed in a plane crash in the Soviet Union on their way to get immigration papers for the trip to America; she came alone with her young son. Twenty-one years ago he broke his neck in a diving accident and was left a quadriplegic. Twenty-one years ago her brother was killed in El Salvador.

Teddington Hamm (Ted) Moy. September 10 was his wife's fiftieth birthday.

Christopher Mozzillo, firefighter, Engine 55. **Stephen Vincent W. Mulderry. Richard Muldowney Jr.,** firefighter, Ladder 7. **Michael Dermott Mullan,** firefighter, Ladder 12. **Dennis Michael Mulligan,** firefighter, Ladder 2.

Murder.

Peter James Mulligan. On September 11, he had been married for almost four months.

Michael Joseph Mullin. James Donald Munhall. Nancy Muniz. Carlos Mario Munoz. Frank Munoz. Theresa (Terry) Munson. Robert M. Murach. Cesar Augusto Murillo. Marc A. Murolo. Brian Joseph Murphy. Charles Anthony Murphy.

The new house. On Monday after work she met her husband at the lawyer's office and they signed the papers. They would take possession in thirty days. Afterward they went out for dinner to celebrate. Then they went home and thought about packing and what color would they paint the new kitchen and where would they put the piano?

Christopher William White Murphy. On September 11, his second child, a girl, was five months old.

Edward Charles Murphy. September 25 was his forty-third birthday.

James Francis Murphy IV.

On the desk. A trophy from last year's company golf tournament engraved with his name, his score, and the date. A clear glass paperweight with a real golf ball inside. A pencil holder in the shape of a golf bag. A *Far Side* desk calendar. Eight fiftieth-birthday cards from his colleagues, all of them humorous, featuring over-the-hill jokes and funny lines about losing your hair, your car keys, your brain cells, your sex drive.

James Thomas Murphy. Expectant father. His third child, a girl, was born on February 1, 2002.

Kevin James Murphy. September 8 was his fortieth birthday.

Lieutenant Commander Patrick Jude Murphy. Patrick Sean Murphy. Lieutenant Raymond E. Murphy, firefighter, Ladder 16. **Robert Eddie Murphy Jr. John J. Murray.**

The things they loved. He loved shooting pistols at the gun range. She loved wood carving. He loved taking his daughter to the airport to watch the planes. She loved boxing. He loved politics. She loved the Washington Redskins. He loved the Oakland Raiders. She loved the Montreal Canadiens. He loved the Three Stooges. She loved Bugs Bunny. He loved riding motorcycles. She loved horror movies. He loved playing the trombone. She loved being a Brownie and Girl Scout leader. He loved smoking Cohiba cigars. She loved taking an annual cruise to the Bahamas. He loved singing a cappella. She loved playing the slot machines in Atlantic City. He loved Aerosmith. She loved Madonna. He loved KISS. She loved Diana Ross. He loved Bob Dylan. She loved Tina Turner. He loved classical Indian music. She loved Andrés Segovia. He loved Barry White.

John Joseph (Jack) Murray Jr. On September 11, his first child, a girl, was five months old. September 18 was his thirty-third birthday.

Susan D. Murray.

At 10:45 a.m. all federal office buildings in Washington, D.C., are evacuated.

Valaria Victoria Murray. September 15 was her sixty-sixth birthday.

Richard Todd Myhre.

Star light, star bright. On a clear night she often stood in the backyard and looked up until her neck ached. *First star I see tonight.* She watched and she wished. She named the constellations out loud in the night: Ursa Major, Ursa Minor, Orion, Pegasus, Perseus, Cassiopeia. *I wish I may, I wish I might.* Even if she couldn't see them, she knew they were there: Canis Major, Canis Minor, Corona Borealis, Andromeda, Hercules, Phoenix. *Have the wish I wish tonight.* The moon, called *Luna* by the Romans, *Selene* and *Artemis* by the Greeks, *Quamar* in Arabic, *L'vbawnoh* in Hebrew. Earth's one moon and how many stars? She'd read estimates of 160 billion, 250 billion, 400 billion, a trillion. Nobody knew for sure. Perhaps it was enough just to know that they were always there.

N

Louis J. Nacke. September 9 was his forty-second birthday. September 16 was his first wedding anniversary.

Lieutenant Robert B. Nagel, firefighter, Engine 58.

Red means stop, green means go. The little boy was learning how to cross the street alone. He had the red and green parts all figured out, but yellow was still confusing. He got distracted, thinking about yellow things: dandelions, his favorite shirt, jelly beans, a beach ball, the tall nodding sunflowers at his aunt's house in the country. He reached for his father's hand and his father explained it all again, but the little boy was thinking about the big yellow school bus he would have to get on in the morning for his very first day of school.

Mildred Rose Naiman. September 11 was her son's fifty-eighth birthday.

Takuya Nakamura. Alexander J. R. Napier Jr. Frank Joseph Naples III. John P. Napolitano, firefighter, Rescue 2; posthumously promoted to lieutenant. **Catherine Ann Nardella. Mario Nardone Jr. Manika K. Narula.**

On Monday evening she went shopping. She bought a copper-colored satin shirt that she would wear to work tomorrow with her black suede skirt.

Shawn M. Nassaney. Boyfriend of **Lynn Catherine Goodchild,** also killed. They were traveling to Maui for a four-day vacation before returning to college.

Narender Nath. Karen Susan Navarro. Joseph Michael Navas, police officer, Port Authority. **Francis Joseph Nazario. Glenroy I. (Glenn) Neblett. Marcus Rayman Neblett. Jerome O. Nedd. Laurence Nedell.**

On the desk. A green blotter, a computer, three telephones, a clock radio, a black halogen lamp, a yellow lined notepad, two black and silver mechanical pencils, a tidy stack of files, a clear plastic ruler, a box of paper clips, and not one single personal item.

Luke G. Nee. September 11 was his nineteenth wedding anniversary.

Pete Negron. Laurie Ann Neira. Ann Nicole Nelson. David William Nelson. James Arthur Nelson, police officer, Port Authority. **Michele Ann Nelson.**

NASDAQ trader. Network engineer. Nurse.

Peter Allen Nelson, firefighter, Rescue 4. On September 11, he had been married for three weeks. Expectant father. His third child, a girl, was born on October 6, 2001, three hours after his memorial service.

Theresa (Ginger) Risco Nelson. Oscar Francis Nesbitt. Gerard Terence Nevins, firefighter, Rescue 1.

Firehouse. The rookies peeled the potatoes, chopped the onions, and did the dishes. The other men took turns in the kitchen, which was appropriately equipped with battalion-sized pots and pans. Some men cooked efficiently and economically; others performed their culinary feats with flamboyant abandon, managing to dirty every dish in the house. Each man had his specialty: lasagna, sauerbraten, chili, goulash, spaghetti, Thai chicken curry, tofu and vegetables (no, please, not again!). Once in a while they splurged and ordered takeout, usually Chinese food or pizza. On special occasions, like an anniversary of ten or twenty years of service, an impending wedding, a retirement, or a birth, there might be steaks, shrimp, roast beef, chocolate mousse or cheesecake for dessert. If they were lucky enough to have a genuine chef in the house, there might be jambalaya and tiramisu.

Renée Lucille Newell. Friend of **Carol Marie Bouchard,** also killed.

Christopher C. Newton. Christopher Newton-Carter. Nancy Yuen Ngo. Khang-Ngoc Nguyen. Jody Tepedino Nichilo. Kathleen Ann Nicosia, flight attendant, American Airlines Flight 11.

In training. Now that she had retired after four decades at the bank, she made it a point to keep fit. She walked three miles a day. She thought of this as her training for her weekly bus trip into Manhattan. She needed to keep up her stamina for these long days of shopping in the city with her sister-in-law, days of miles of walking and hunting for bargains, punctuated by lunch at Lord & Taylor, and sometimes a visit to Paulette's Place of Beauty or Connie's Nail Salon.

Martin Stewart Niederer. September 26 was his twenty-fourth birthday.

Alfonse Joseph Niedermeyer III, police officer, Port Authority. Expectant father. His wife found out she was pregnant with their second child a week after his memorial service. The baby, a girl, was born on June 7, 2002.

Frank John Niestadt Jr. Gloria Nieves. Juan Nieves Jr. Troy Edward Nilsen. Paul R. Nimbley. John Ballantine Niven.

Lucky. Much as he knew it was a cliché, still he considered himself lucky to be living the quintessential suburban life. The house was a four-bedroom split-level with an attached double garage. He loved mowing the lawn, trimming the roses, cleaning the gutters, setting up the basketball net in the driveway in the spring, making a small skating rink in the backyard in the winter. The hulking black gas barbecue on the back deck was the size of a small car. He loved grilling burgers and steaks in his long red apron and his silly white chef's hat. The minivan was silver with air-conditioning, a CD player, and a VCR. He loved driving his kids to soccer practice, dance recitals, karate, and piano lessons. He even loved driving them to the mall.

Katherine (Katie) McGarry Noack. On September 11, she had been married for six months.

Curtis Terrence Noel. Boyfriend of **Aisha Anne Harris,** also killed.

Petty Officer Second Class Michael Allen Noeth. Daniel Robert Nolan. Robert Walter Noonan.

Weather. She loved an overnight snowfall, so that even before she looked outside in the morning she knew it had snowed because the light behind the curtains was so white and the silence was more silent than usual, deeper, softer, and thick. An hour later the silence would be replaced by the sound of shovels all up and down the block, and she loved that, too.

Robert Grant Norton. Jacqueline June Norton. Husband and wife. They were flying to California for her son's wedding. Robert was the oldest person to die on September 11. He was eighty-five.

Daniela R. Notaro.

Souvenirs. They were kept in a special drawer, dated and wrapped in tissue paper. They belonged to her parents, mementos of trips they had made before they became her parents. 1948: a black velvet cushion with a picture of Niagara Falls, where they had gone for their honeymoon. 1949: a snow globe of Mount Rushmore. 1950: a tea towel from Florida printed with a sailfish, a map, and a calendar. 1951: a miniature bronze replica of the Golden Gate Bridge. 1952: a set of four highball glasses featuring images of the Statue of Liberty, the Empire State Building, the Chrysler Building, and the Brooklyn Bridge. After she and her three brothers were born, her parents had given up traveling. After her parents both died of cancer in the same year, she did not know what else to do with these souvenirs except keep them.

Brian Christopher Novotny. He became engaged on September 4, 2001.

Soichi Numata. Brian Felix Nuñez. José R. Nuñez. Jeffrey Roger Nussbaum.

Night.

O

Dennis Patrick O'Berg, firefighter, Ladder 105.

On Monday evening they watched TV, mostly clicking through the channels, complaining about the reruns and saying how much they were looking forward to the start of the new fall season, which seemed to come a little later every year.

James Patrick O'Brien Jr. On September 11, his first child, a boy, was five weeks old.

Michael P. O'Brien. Scott J. O'Brien.

Collapsed buildings:

1 World Trade Center
2 World Trade Center
5 World Trade Center
7 World Trade Center
North Bridge, pedestrian walkway over West Street connecting the World Trade Center to the World Financial Center.

Timothy Michael O'Brien. Brother-in-law of **Stephen Edward Tighe,** also killed.

Lieutenant Daniel O'Callaghan, firefighter, Ladder 4. **Dennis James O'Connor Jr.**

At 10:54 a.m. Israel evacuates all diplomatic missions.

Diana J. Vega O'Connor. She was the second youngest in a family of sixteen children.

Keith Kevin O'Connor. Richard J. O'Connor. Amy O'Doherty. Marni Pont O'Doherty.

Distinguishing features. Staple scar on his lower back, scar from hernia operation on his lower abdomen, scar on right index finger, laproscopic scar near his belly button. Right breast removed. Two front teeth slightly protruding; small feet, possibly painted toenails. Open-heart surgery scar on his chest. Smallpox vaccination mark on her left arm. Two fingers missing on his right hand. Surgical scarring on both knees, short fingers and toes. Six feet, two inches tall; nearly four hundred pounds. Scar from her hip to her thigh on either right or left side. Light scar on his upper lip, three-inch scar on his stomach. Port wine stain birthmark on her inner ankle. Insulin pump in abdomen (firm to the touch).

James Andrew O'Grady. On September 11, he had been engaged for five weeks.

Lieutenant Thomas G. O'Hagan, firefighter, Battalion 4. **Patrick J. O'Keefe,** firefighter, Rescue 1. **Captain William O'Keefe,** firefighter, Division 15.

Oblivion.

Gerald Thomas O'Leary. Brother-in-law of **Robert Garvin McCarthy,** also killed. September 28 was his son's first birthday.

Matthew Timothy O'Mahony. Seamus L. O'Neal.

In the refrigerator. Three half-empty containers of Chinese food and four little packets of plum sauce. A carton of milk three days past its expiration date. A bottle of blue Gatorade. Small jars of instant coffee, mayonnaise, mustard, and strawberry jam. A loaf of white bread. Bottles of ketchup, salad dressing, soy sauce, and maple syrup. Two bruised apples. A package of wieners. Six cans of Coke. Eight cans of Bud Light. Something unrecognizable in a plastic bag pushed to the very back. In the freezer compartment, two empty ice cube trays, six single-serving microwave meals, a tub of maple walnut ice cream, a sausage pizza, and one buttermilk waffle gone furry with freezer burn. He knew this was pathetic. He knew he could do better. But oh, he was so busy, so inept in the kitchen, and so tired of living alone.

John P. O'Neill Sr., chief of security for the World Trade Center, former head of the FBI's counterterrorism division. He was to retire at the end of September.

Peter J. O'Neill Jr.

Works of art worth an estimated $100 million were destroyed, including pieces by Pablo Picasso, David Hockney, Roy Lichtenstein, Ross Bleckner, Le Corbusier, and Paul Klee. Citigroup Corporation lost 1,113 pieces of art, including works by Carl Schrag, Louis Bouche, John Heilker, William Thon, Romare Bearden, Jacob Lawrence, Jim Dine, and Currier and Ives. Also lost: a collection of 25 rare antique handwoven kilim rugs worth more than $500,000; a portion of the Broadway Theatre Archive's 35,000 photographs of great moments in the history of the American stage; 40,000 negatives of photographs by Jacques Lowe documenting the presidency of JFK.

Sean Gordon Corbett O'Neill. On September 11, he had been married for three months. Expectant father. His first child, a girl, was born on March 8, 2002.

Kevin M. O'Rourke, firefighter, Rescue 2. **Patrick J. O'Shea. Robert William O'Shea. Timothy F. O'Sullivan. James A. Oakley.**

On the back of the bathroom door, hanging from two brass hooks above the full-length mirror, there was a pair of red plaid pajamas and a royal blue velour bathrobe patterned with red and yellow stars and moons. On the floor in the corner behind the door, there was a pair of beaded butterscotch leather moccasins so worn that the left one had a hole in the sole.

Douglas E. Oelschlager, firefighter, Ladder 15. On September 11, he was thirty-six years old. Both his father and his grandfather had died at the age of thirty-six.

Takashi Ogawa. Albert Ogletree. Philip Paul Ognibene. Captain John Ogonowski, pilot, American Airlines Flight 11. **Joseph J. (Jay) Ogren,** firefighter, Ladder 3. **Samuel Oitice,** firefighter, Ladder 4. **Gerald Michael Olcott. Christine Anne Olender. Linda Mary Oliva.**

Secrets. He had served in the army in Vietnam. He had been awarded the Bronze Star for valor. He would not discuss his memories of the war with anyone, not even his wife. He had seen things no one should ever have to see. He did not want to remember. He had survived, his friends had not, and that was all he knew for sure. He did not know why.

Edward Kraft Oliver. On September 11, his second child, a boy, was four months old.

Leah E. Oliver. September 12 was her twenty-fifth birthday.

Eric Taube Olsen, firefighter, Ladder 15. **Jeffrey James Olsen,** firefighter, Engine 10. **Barbara Kay Bracher Olson. Maureen Lyons Olson. Steven John Olson,** firefighter, Ladder 3.

At 10:57 a.m. all New York State government offices are closed.

Toshihiro Onda. Betty Ann Ong, flight attendant, American Airlines Flight 11. **Michael C. Opperman. Christopher T. Orgielewicz. Margaret Quinn Orloske. Virginia Anne Ormiston-Kenworthy.**

Office manager. Office renovator. Operations manager.

Ruben S. Ornedo. On September 11, he had been married for three months. Expectant father. His first child, a girl, was born on January 31, 2002.

Ronald Orsini. Peter K. Ortale. Jane Marie Iaci Orth. Alexander Ortiz. David Ortiz.

A room with a view. What the investment banker loved the most about his new office on the 104th floor was the view. On a clear day he could see for fifty miles. The whole of the city was spread out below him. He could see the top of the Empire State Building, the George Washington Bridge, and the shadows of the towers themselves. With the help of binoculars he could even pick out his own boat moored in the river, a thirty-eight-foot cruiser he had bought in July and named after his wife. What surprised him the most was how green the city was from this vantage point. He was especially tickled when he looked out on the second morning and saw a small plane flying below him.

Emilio (Peter) Ortiz Jr. On September 14, his twin daughters were six months old.

Pablo Ortiz. Paul Ortiz Jr. Sonia Ortiz. Masaru Ose. Elsy Carolina Osorio-Oliva. James Robert Ostrowski. Jason Douglas Oswald. Michael J. Otten, firefighter, Ladder 35. **Isidro D. Ottenwalder. Michael Chung Ou. Todd Joseph Ouida. Jesus Ovalles. Peter J. Owens Jr. Adianes Oyola.**

Last seen wearing. Raymond Weil watch, two-carat diamond solitaire ring, pearl earrings. Medic Alert bracelet on his right wrist, yellow-gold wedding band engraved *9/22/79 DAW,* signet ring on his right hand engraved *MSH.* Barbell-shaped earring in one ear, three tiny hoops in the other. FDNY ring, gold with red Maltese cross and unit number. Wedding band engraved *Rich, All My Love, Maura.* Silver Tag watch on his right wrist, gold chain with two charms: a small camera and a picture of his daughters. Wedding band engraved *Till Death;* his wife's ring read *Do Us Part.*

P

Angel M. (Chic) Pabón. Israel Pabon Jr. Roland Pacheco. Michael Benjamin Packer. Diana B. Padro. Deepa K. Pakkala.

The end of the day. As he walked up the road from the train station each day at six o'clock, the risk manager knew that his wife, his baby daughter, and the dog would be sitting on the stoop waiting for him. He knew that no matter how tired and cranky he was, the minute he caught sight of them, his spirits would lift. Pulling off his tie and stuffing it into his jacket pocket, he would start to walk faster. He knew that by the time the dog rushed into the road to greet him, he would be waving and humming. After supper they would put the baby in the stroller and take a walk around the neighborhood with the dog galloping ahead, greeting everyone they met (four-legged or two) with the same joyful, tail-wagging exuberance.

Jeffrey Matthew Palazzo, firefighter, Rescue 5. September 15 was his eleventh wedding anniversary.

Thomas Anthony Palazzo. Richard A. (Rico) Palazzolo. Orio Joseph Palmer, firefighter, deputy chief, Battalion 7; posthumously promoted to battalion chief.

Anniversary dinner. Mixed greens and mandarin salad, grilled lamb chops with mashed chickpeas and sautéed seasonal vegetables. There were white candles on the table, much sparkling stemware and silverware, gold-rimmed plates, a dozen red roses and a pair of diamond earrings in a velvet box from him to her, a black walnut fly box containing twenty-four hand-tied fishing flies from England from her to him. They toasted themselves several times, proud of having made it to the ten-year mark when so many of their friends had not, had been divorced already, some more than once. They called the babysitter to make sure everything was fine at home, and then they ordered chocolate raspberry cheesecake for dessert.

Frank Anthony Palombo, firefighter, Ladder 105. He was the father of ten children.

Alan N. Palumbo. September 13 was his forty-third birthday.

Christopher Matthew Panatier. Dominique Lisa Pandolfo. Lieutenant Jonas Martin Panik. Paul J. Pansini, firefighter, Engine 10; posthumously promoted to fire marshal. **John M. Paolillo,** firefighter, deputy chief, Battalion 11; posthumously promoted to battalion chief. **Edward Joseph Papa. Salvatore T. Papasso.**

On Monday night the editorial director stayed up late preparing for an important meeting first thing in the morning.

James Nicholas Pappageorge, firefighter, Engine 23. He had been on the job for six weeks.

Marie Pappalardo.

Breaking News. He had to admit he was addicted to CNN. It had all started with O. J., with watching that white Bronco racing down the freeway for hours. He could not look away. Now, whenever a dramatic event was unfolding live before him on the screen, he was utterly mesmerized. He was riveted while they cut from the action to various on-the-scene reporters quoting their secret sources and to a plethora of experts analyzing, speculating, and analyzing some more. Even when they replayed the same footage a dozen times in an hour, he was still hooked. He was ashamed to admit that by the end of a slow news week, he sometimes caught himself secretly longing for a good car chase, a horrendous crime, or a five-alarm fire.

Vinod Kumar Parakat. Expectant father. His first child was due in December 2001.

Vijayashanker Paramsothy. Best friend and protégé of **Howard L. Kestenbaum,** also killed.

Nitin Ramesh Parandter. Hardai (Casey) Parbhu. James Wendell Parham, police officer, Port Authority. **Debra Marie Paris.**

Favorite television shows. *The Simpsons. The X-Files. Jeopardy! Survivor. Star Trek. Judge Judy. The Young and the Restless. General Hospital. Melrose Place. Wheel of Fortune. Saturday Night Live. Touched by an Angel. Little House on the Prairie. Everybody Loves Raymond. Friends. Good Times. Full House. Three's Company. The Munsters. The Honeymooners. Bonanza. Seinfeld. Oprah. Taxi. CHiPS. Sesame Street. Iron Chef. Emeril Live. Trading Spaces. Who Wants to Be a Millionaire. The West Wing. NYPD Blue. Law & Order.*

George Paris. On September 11, his first child, a girl, was six months old.

Gye-Hong Park. Philip Lacey Parker. Michael Alaine Parkes. Robert Emmett Parks Jr. Hashmukhrai Chuckulal Parmar. Robert Parro, firefighter, Engine 8. **Diane Marie Moore Parsons.**

Former lives. Thirty years ago, addicted to heroin, he lost his wife, his son, and his job. He went to prison for a robbery conviction. When he was released, he moved in with his parents and found another job. But they died and he was evicted, and then he lost his job again. He was homeless for the next ten years, sleeping in a Harlem shelter or on the sidewalk near Grand Central Terminal. But then, with the help of various social service agencies, he started to turn his life around. He found a place to live and got a steady job at the World Trade Center. He had worked there for three years.

Leobardo Lopez Pascual. Best friend of **Antonio Melendez,** also killed.

Michael J. Pascuma Jr. Jerrold H. Paskins. Horace Robert Passananti. Suzanne H. Passaro.

Panic.

Avnish Ramanbhai Patel. Dipti Patel. Manish K. Patel. Steven Bennett Paterson.

The things they loved. She loved her crystal fox fur coat and matching hat. He loved his Harley-Davidson, a burnt-orange 1340-cc Heritage model. She loved her red Chrysler Sebring convertible. He loved his black BMW 740iL, maximum speed 156 mph, 0 to 60 in 6.8 seconds. She loved her 1966 baby-blue Volkwagen Bug. He loved his Sunbeam Alpine, his MG Midget, and, especially, his yellow Morgan roadster. She loved her Sub-Zero refrigerator, built-in with wood paneling so it looked like part of the cabinetry. He loved his black titanium golf clubs. She loved her Salomon X Scream downhill skis.

James Matthew Patrick. Expectant father. His first child, a boy, was born on October 11, 2001.

Manuel D. Patrocino. Bernard E. Patterson. Captain Clifford Leon Patterson Jr., posthumously promoted to major. **Cira Marie Patti. Robert Edward Pattison. James Robert Paul. Patrice Sobin Paz. Victor Paz-Gutiérrez.**

The things they loved. He loved his Black and Decker table saw. She loved her DeLonghi retro espresso and cappuccino maker. He loved his 57-inch big-screen projection TV. She loved her Italian marble bathroom sink. He loved his Sony PlayStation 2. She loved her 1900 Galle Cameo Vase, 24 inches tall, triple-layered glass in purple-plum over crystal over frosted white, acid-etched and fire-polished in a floral pattern similar to a passion flower, the first of what she hoped would eventually become a substantial collection.

Stacey Lynn Peak. September 4 was her thirty-sixth birthday.

Richard Allen Pearlman, volunteer medic. **Durrell V. Pearsall Jr.,** firefighter, Rescue 4.

Recovered: 4 autographed baseballs.

Thomas Nicholas Pecorelli. Expectant father. His first child, a boy, was born on March 19, 2002.

Thomas E. Pedicini. Brother-in-law of **Mark Joseph Colaio,** also killed.

Todd Douglas Pelino. Brother-in-law of **Kaleen Elizabeth Pezzuti,** also killed.

Michel Adrian Pelletier. On September 11, his second child, a boy, was three months old.

Anthony G. Peluso. Angel Ramon Pena. Robert Penniger. Richard Al Penny. Salvatore F. Pepe. Carl Allen Peralta. Robert David Peraza.

Partially collapsed buildings:

1 Liberty Plaza
4 World Trade Center
6 World Trade Center
Marriott Financial Center Hotel

Jon A. Perconti Jr. Expectant father. His first child, a girl, was born on December 8, 2001.

Alejo Perez. Angel Perez Jr. Angela Susan Perez. Anthony Perez.

On Tuesday afternoon the personal banker was going to take the bull by the horns, so to speak, and tell that obnoxious new client she couldn't work with him anymore.

Ivan A. Perez. Fiancé of **Eileen Flecha,** also killed.

Nancy E. Perez. Berinthia (Berry) Berenson Perkins. Joseph John Perroncino. Edward Joseph Perrotta. Emelda H. Perry. Lieutenant Glenn C. Perry, firefighter, Ladder 25.

On Tuesday afternoon the file clerk was going to clean out her own messy desk once and for all, and then she was going to keep it perfectly tidy and organized forever.

John William Perry, police officer, NYPD. On September 11, he was filing his resignation papers, planning to become a medical malpractice lawyer.

Franklin Allan Pershep. Daniel Pesce.

On Tuesday afternoon the margins clerk was going to master that incomprehensible new computer program if it was the last thing he did.

Michael John Pescherine. Expectant father. His first child, a boy, was born on February 3, 2002.

Davin Peterson. His younger sister's boyfriend, **Frederick John Cox,** was also killed.

Donald Arthur Peterson. Jean Hoadley Peterson. Husband and wife. On September 11, their first grandchild, a girl, was two and a half weeks old.

William Russell Peterson.

Painter. Pastry maker. Pastry sous chef. Pediatrician (retired). Personal assistant. Personal banker. Personal driver. Personal policy integrator. Philanthropist. Photographer. Physician. Physicist. Pizza delivery boy. Political commentator. Porter. Post commander. Prep cook. President. Priest. Professor. Program analyst. Psychologist. Publisher.

Mark Petrocelli. September 13 was his twenty-ninth birthday.

Lieutenant Philip Scott Petti, firefighter, Battalion 7. **Glen Kerrin Pettit,** police officer, NYPD. **Dominick A. Pezzulo,** police officer, Port Authority.

Police. He had once talked a jilted lover down from a ledge on the George Washington Bridge. He had once wrestled a deranged gunman into a straitjacket before he could hurt anyone. He had once rescued a boy who was trapped in an elevator with his head wedged between a beam and the car. He had spent a year defusing land mines in Bosnia as a volunteer member of a United Nations international police force. In 1991 she had saved dozens of lives in the subway crash at Union Square that left 5 people dead and more than 130 injured. In 1992 he had rushed into a burning jumbo jet that had crashed on takeoff at Kennedy Airport and helped save all 292 passengers aboard.

Kaleen Elizabeth Pezzuti. Girlfriend of **Matthew James Grzymalski,** also killed. Sister-in-law of **Todd Douglas Pelino,** also killed.

Lieutenant Kevin Pfeifer, firefighter, Engine 33.

Passion.

Tu-Anh Pham. On September 10, she returned to work after a six-week maternity leave. Her first child, a girl, was born in July 2001.

Lieutenant Kenneth John Phelan, firefighter, Engine 217. **Suzette Eugenia Piantieri. Ludwig John Picarro. Matthew M. Picerno. Joseph Oswald Pick. Christopher Pickford,** firefighter, Engine 201. **Dennis J. Pierce. Bernard T. Pietronico. Nicholas P. Pietrunti. Theodoros Pigis. Susan Elizabeth Ancona Pinto. Joseph Piskadlo. Christopher Todd Pitman.**

At 11:02 a.m. New York City mayor Rudolph Giuliani orders the evacuation of Lower Manhattan south of Canal Street.

Joshua M. Piver. Friend of **Eric Thomas Ropiteau,** also killed. On September 10, they had signed the lease for a large apartment with two other friends.

Robert R. Ploger III. Zandra F. Cooper Ploger. Husband and wife. On September 11, they had been married for four months. They were flying to Hawaii for their honeymoon.

Joseph Plumitallo. John Michael Pocher. William Howard Pohlmann. Laurence Michael Polatsch. Thomas H. Polhemus. Steve Pollicino. Susan M. Pollio. Lieutenant J. G. Darin Howard Pontell. Joshua Iousa Poptean. Giovanna Porras. Anthony Portillo. James Edward Potorti. Daphne Pouletsos.

In the dream someone had died, although no one was saying who or how or when. But as they do when they don't know what else to do about death, people were bringing food, more food, mountains of food. Loaves of bread, bags of apples, turkeys both raw and cooked, a side of beef, a hundred tuna casseroles, a thousand chocolate cakes. No one could eat fast enough. Still it kept coming. Soon they were buried up to their necks in food. Soon they could not breathe, and the food was rotting all around them.

Richard N. Poulos. Brother-in-law of **James Patrick Hopper,** also killed.

Stephen Emanual Poulos. Brandon Jerome Powell. Scott Powell. Shawn Edward Powell, firefighter, Engine 207. **Antonio Pratt. Gregory M. Preziose.**

What remains. Twenty-three photo albums. Twenty-one hand-carved pipes. Twenty small statues of the Virgin Mary. Nineteen umbrellas. Sixteen pairs of black shoes. Fifteen pairs of prescription eyeglasses. Fourteen Brooks Brothers suits. Thirteen antique coffeepots. Twelve fishing rods. Eleven bathrobes. Eleven antique vehicles, including several Cadillacs from the 1940s and one old fire engine.

Wanda Ivelisse Astol Prince. September 10 was her second wedding anniversary.

Vincent A. Princiotta, firefighter, Ladder 7. **Kevin M. Prior,** firefighter, Squad 252. **Everett Martin (Marty) Proctor III. Carrie Beth Progen. David Lee Pruim. Richard Prunty,** firefighter, chief, Battalion 2. **John Foster Puckett. Robert David Pugliese.**

Favorite foods. Honey-glazed turkey. Eggplant parmigiana. Cheeseburgers. Chocolate mousse cake. Spinach lasagna. Canned mackerel. Fried chicken. Jalapeño jelly. Mashed potatoes. Barbecued shrimp. French toast. Key lime pie. Clam chowder. Popcorn. Twizzlers. Arroz con gandules. Cod and potatoes in creole sauce. Curried goat. Apple-pecan blintzes. Chocolate-covered strawberries. Banana pudding. Ziti. Krispy Kreme doughnuts.

Edward F. Pullis. September 11 was his wife's thirty-third birthday.

Patricia Ann Puma. Captain Jack D. Punches (retired). Sonia Mercedes Morales Puopolo. Hemanth Kumar Puttur. Petty Officer First Class Joseph John Pycior Jr. Edward Richard Pykon.

Las Vegas. They went for a weekend in August. It was their first visit: from one city that never sleeps to another; from Gotham to Sin City, from the Big Apple to the City of Lights, America's Playground. The young man was dazzled by the neon, the music, the free drinks, the all-day-all-night excitement. Swept away by his own impulsive romanticism, he wanted to get married right then and there. But the young woman, more cautious and practical by nature, insisted that they wait and do it properly, with their family and friends, a white gown, a cake, and a honeymoon. The young man was disappointed, but what could he do? So they went home still unmarried but ready to set a date and make a plan.

Q

Christopher Quackenbush. Lars Peter Qualben. Lincoln Quappé, firefighter, Rescue 2. **Beth Ann Quigley.**

On Monday night they made love for what must have been the thousandth time.

Patrick J. Quigley IV. Expectant father. His second child, a girl, was born on October 15, 2001.

Lieutenant Michael Thomas Quilty, firefighter, Ladder 11. On September 5, he celebrated his twentieth anniversary with the FDNY.

James Francis Quinn. Lieutenant Ricardo J. Quinn, FDNY paramedic, Battalion 57; posthumously promoted to lieutenant.

Quiet.

R

Carol Millicent Rabalais.

The past. Twenty years ago he broke his nose, collarbone, and several ribs while playing rugby. Twenty years ago he was orphaned at the age of fifteen. Twenty years ago he ran through a plate-glass window and required more than a hundred stitches. Twenty years ago her husband was murdered during an armed robbery. Twenty years ago she grew up in Iran near a border under heavy bombardment by Iraq. Eighteen years ago, while serving as a soldier in Grenada, he broke his back in a crash that destroyed three helicopters. Sixteen years ago, when he was eighteen, he was severely burned when a pot of oil on the stove caught fire and exploded.

Christopher Peter A. Racaniello. He was to be married on November 24, 2001.

Leonard J. Ragaglia, firefighter, Engine 54. **Eugene J. Raggio. Laura Marie Ragonese-Snik. Michael Paul Ragusa,** firefighter, Engine 279. **Peter Frank Raimondi.**

At 11:45 a.m. President Bush arrives at Barksdale Air Force Base in Louisiana. The American military is on nuclear alert.

Harry A. Raines. September 15 was his thirty-eighth birthday.

Lisa J. Raines. Ehtesham U. Raja. Valsa Raju. Edward J. Rall, firefighter, Rescue 2. **Lucas (Luke) Rambousek. Maria Isabel Ramirez. Harry Ramos.**

Buildings that suffered major damage:

3 World Financial Center (American Express)

90 West Street

Bankers Trust Building at 130 Liberty Street

East River Savings Bank

Saint Nicholas Greek Orthodox Church

South Bridge, pedestrian walkway over West Street

U.S. Federal Building at 90 Church Street

Vishnoo Ramsaroop. He was the father of eight children.

Deborah A. Ramsaur. Lorenzo E. Ramzey. Alfred Todd Rancke. Adam David Rand, firefighter, Squad 288. **Jonathan C. Randall. Srinivasa Shreyas Ranganath. Anne Rose T. Ransom. Faina Aronovna Rapoport. Rhonda Sue Ridge Rasmussen. Robert Arthur Rasmussen. Amenia Rasool. Roger Mark Rasweiler. Petty Officer First Class Marsha Dianah Ratchford. David Alan James Rathkey.**

When they saw the baby on the sonogram, it was happily sucking its thumb. They did not want to know if it was a boy or a girl, preferring to be surprised in the old-fashioned way. They took the picture home and put it on the fridge door. With only one month to go, they had finished decorating the nursery and were buying diapers, sleepers, and adorable stuffed toys. They bought a musical mobile to hang over the crib. Her mother was planning to have a baby shower in late October after the baby was born. She was superstitious and believed it was bad luck to have the shower beforehand.

William Ralph Raub. On September 11, his second child, a boy, was three months old.

Gerard P. Rauzi. Alexey Razuvaev.

Regrets. If she had it to do over again, she would do it all differently. But it seemed too late now to make those kinds of big changes that could get her life moving in a new direction.

Gregory Reda. On September 11, his second child, a boy, was two months old.

Sarah Prothero Redheffer. Michele Marie Reed. Judith Ann Reese.

No regrets. If he had it to do over again, he wouldn't change a single thing. He harbored no regrets for any of the things he had done, nor for the things he hadn't. He didn't know which part of this was more important, but he did know it was unusual.

Donald J. Regan, firefighter, Rescue 3. **Lieutenant Robert M. Regan,** firefighter, Ladder 118. **Thomas Michael Regan.**

Distinguishing features: tattoos. Small green fire-breathing dragon on his right upper arm. Blue rose on her left ankle. Leaping tiger on his left forearm. Eagle and American flag on his upper right arm. Large green and black fish on her lower back. Howling wolf on his right wrist. Saint Michael the archangel on his right shoulder blade; Saint Anthony, patron of lost things, on his left arm; also on his left arm, surrounded by cherubs, the Serenity Prayer: *God grant me the serenity to accept the things I cannot change, the courage to change the things I can, and the wisdom to know the difference.*

Christian Michael Otto Regenhard, firefighter, Ladder 131. He had been on the job for six weeks.

Howard Reich. Gregg Reidy. James Brian Reilly.

At 12:04 p.m. Los Angeles International Airport is evacuated.

Kevin Owen Reilly, firefighter, Engine 207. On September 11, he had been married for two months.

Timothy Edward Reilly.

Crazy for cats. Although her apartment was hardly big enough to swing a cat in (as her brother said far too often), still the young woman could not resist taking in the strays that showed up regularly on her doorstep, as if word of her hospitality were being passed through the cat community in some surreptitious feline code. The number of cats in residence was now at seventeen. There were four tabbies, three pure black, two pure white, two orange, one pregnant Siamese, and five others best described as miscellaneous. Once ensconced, named, and given its own bowl and blanket, each new arrival seemed happy to leave the street life behind and wallow in this little haven of comfortable (if crowded) domesticity. The cats were apparently as grateful for her hospitality as she was for their company.

Joseph Reina Jr. Expectant father. His first child, a boy, was born on October 4, 2001.

Thomas Barnes Reinig. Frank Bennett Reisman. Joshua Scott Reiss. Karen C. Renda.

Writing a poem. The disaster recovery specialist had never written a poem in his life before and had no idea why he seemed to be writing one now. He had only one line so far. He didn't know if it was the first line, the last line, or from somewhere in the middle. This line had been stuck in his head for days like a line of music that plays in your brain all day long just because you happened to hear it on the car radio on the way to work in the morning. He thought maybe if he wrote it down, then the line would go away. But it did not. Instead it reversed itself so now he had two lines:

We are the living. You are the dead.

You are the living. We are the dead.

He waited for more lines to follow, but they did not.

John Armand Reo. Brother-in-law of **John Francis Swaine,** also killed.

Colonel Richard Cyril Rescorla.

Former lives. Five years ago she was a waitress trapped in an abusive relationship. The future was a black hole she preferred not to think about. Three and a half years ago she changed her life. She began a new relationship with a wonderful man. They got married. She took a job as a temporary secretary for a large financial corporation. Her rise through the ranks of the company was unprecedented and nothing short of meteoric: from secretary to assistant broker to full broker to assistant vice president. Against all odds, she had begun to believe that the worst was over. She could almost allow herself to believe that the best was yet to come.

John Thomas Resta. Sylvia SanPio Resta. Husband and wife. Sylvia was seven months pregnant with their first child.

Martha M. Reszke.

Redemption.

David E. Retik. Expectant father. His third child, a girl, was born on October 19, 2001.

Todd H. Reuben. Luis Clodoaldo Revilla. Eduvigis (Eddie) Reyes Jr. Bruce Albert Reynolds, police officer, Port Authority. **John Frederick Rhodes Jr. Francis Saverio Riccardelli. Rudolph N. Riccio. AnnMarie Davi Riccoboni. David Harlow Rice. Eileen Mary Rice. Kenneth Frederick Rice III.**

The things they carried. Red canvas shoulder bag containing a small Spanish-English dictionary, a deck of playing cards, a roll of quarters, a turquoise plastic rosary. Small box of rocks, a gift from his son. Three packs of Nicorette gum in back pocket. Brand-new digital camera with instruction manual in black leather pouch. Pittsburgh Steelers jersey. Yellow backpack containing a bottle of water, an apple, a peanut butter sandwich, *World of Wrestling* magazine, travel guide to the Channel Islands. Small green purse with gold shoulder strap containing three credit cards, employee ID card, breath mints, and a personal safety alarm. Magnifying glass. Mandolin. Pale green worry stone in left breast pocket. Two tickets to the September 16 performance of *The Producers.*

Cecelia E. Richard. Lieutenant Vernon Allan Richard, firefighter, Ladder 7; posthumously promoted to captain. **Claude Daniel Richards,** detective, bomb squad, NYPD. **Gregory David Richards. Michael Richards. Venesha Orintia Rodgers Richards.**

Grocery list. Written on the back of an envelope from AT&T, stuck to the fridge with a magnet in the shape of a chocolate chip cookie so realistic that visiting children always tried to eat it, the list was a work-in-progress, added to daily in preparation for the weekly trip to the supermarket on Saturday afternoon.

Orange juice	Olives
Ketchup	Lightbulbs
Ice cream	Raisins
Bread	Eggs

James C. Riches, firefighter, Engine 4. September 12 was his thirtieth birthday.

Alan Jay Richman. John M. Rigo. Frederick Charles Rimmele III. Rose Mary Riso. Moises N. Rivas. Joseph Rivelli Jr., firefighter, Ladder 25.

Firehouse. Many of the men moonlighted to make some extra money. They drove taxis, sanded floors, fixed roofs, hung wallpaper, and painted apartments. They worked as bartenders, plumbers, nightclub bouncers, auto mechanics, and engineers. Several of the men worked as models and part-time actors in television and movies. One had played a paramedic in *The Sopranos, Law & Order,* and *Third Watch.* One owned a limousine business on the side, and another drove a hot-dog truck. One was a first-class pastry chef, and another was a popular musician whose band played at weddings and bar mitzvahs. When they weren't working at one job or another, many also served as volunteer firefighters in their home communities.

Carmen Alicia Rivera. Isaias Rivera. Juan William Rivera. Linda Ivelisse Rivera.

Respect.

David E. Rivers. Joseph R. Riverso. Paul V. Rizza. John Frank Rizzo. Stephen Louis Roach.

At 12:15 p.m. American borders with Canada and Mexico are closed.

Joseph Roberto. Expectant father. His second child, a boy, was born on May 5, 2002.

Leo Arthur Roberts. Michael E. Roberts, firefighter, Engine 214. **Michael Edward Roberts,** firefighter, Ladder 35.

Secrets. Every Thanksgiving her large extended family congregated at one house or another for a traditional feast. They ate all the things you're supposed to eat on this occasion, finishing off with slabs of pumpkin pie topped with whipped cream. Every year, as they finally pushed themselves away from the table groaning, she put on her coat and went out. She said she was going to visit a friend. The family was curious, of course, but they knew better than to ask too many questions. She was a very private person. The family could not have guessed that she was going downtown to the soup kitchen to serve Thanksgiving dinner to the homeless.

Donald Walter Robertson Jr. Catharina Robinson. Jeffrey Robinson. Michell Lee Jean Robotham. Donald Arthur Robson. Antonio Augusto Tome Rocha. Raymond James Rocha. Laura Rockefeller. John M. Rodak. Antonio José Carrusca Rodrigues, police officer, Port Authority.

Buildings that suffered serious structural damage:

1 World Financial Center
2 World Financial Center
4 World Financial Center
14 Wall Street
30 West Broadway

Millenium Hilton Hotel
New York Telephone Building (Verizon Communications)
Winter Garden

Anthony Rodriguez, firefighter, Engine 279. Expectant father. His sixth child, a girl, was born on September 14, 2001.

Carmen Milagros Rodriguez. Gregory Ernesto Rodriguez. Marsha A. Rodriguez. Richard Rodriguez, police officer, Port Authority. **David Bartolo Rodriguez-Vargas.**

At 12:15 p.m. San Francisco International Airport is evacuated.

Matthew Rogan, firefighter, Ladder 11. **Jean Destrehan Rogér,** flight attendant, American Airlines Flight 11. **Karlie Barbara Rogers. Scott William Rohner. Keith Roma,** firefighter, New York Fire Patrol. **Joseph M. Romagnolo. Efrain Franco Romero Sr. Elvin Santiago Romero. Chief James A. Romito,** police chief, Port Authority. **Sean Paul Rooney.**

Radio communications specialist. Receiving attendant. Receptionist. Recruiter. Recycling-program worker. Research assistant. Reserve officer. Restaurant worker. Risk manager. Rock band representative.

Eric Thomas Ropiteau. Friend of **Joshua M. Piver,** also killed. On September 10, they had signed the lease for a large apartment with two other friends.

Aida Rosario.

On Sunday afternoon they went for a long walk through Central Park. It was unseasonably warm, more like July than September. They wandered through the Shakespeare Garden and then took pictures of each other in front of Belvedere Castle. They commandeered a passing stranger to take a picture of them kissing on the castle steps. Eventually they ended up at Bethesda Fountain. They found a seat on the edge, took off their shoes, and dangled their tired feet in the water. I love you, he said. I love you too, she said. It was the first time they had said it out loud. They had been dating for six months.

Angela Rosario. Fiancée of **Darryl Leron McKinney,** also killed.

Mark Harlan Rosen. Brooke David Rosenbaum. Linda Rosenbaum. Sheryl Lynn Rosner Rosenbaum. Lloyd Daniel Rosenberg. Mark Louis Rosenberg. Andrew Ira Rosenblum.

The things they loved. She loved her grandmother's face in the sunshine, the way the light shone on the fine white hairs dusting her upper lip and her chin, the intricate web of wrinkles crosshatching her cheeks, and the vertical lines deeply etched on both sides of her mouth. He loved his baby daughter's toes, which were as pretty as beads, and he knew he would never have the nerve to trim her nails himself but could only watch and wince while his wife did it with expert ease. She loved her teenage son's shoulders, which were so broad and manly now, yet still so vulnerable, when she was lucky enough to see him coming before he saw her, when she caught a glimpse of him walking away, not knowing that her eyes were on him.

Joshua M. Rosenblum. He was to be married on September 15, 2001.

Joshua Alan Rosenthal. Richard David Rosenthal. Philip Martin Rosenzweig. Richard Barry Ross. Daniel Rossetti.

On Monday evening the commodities trader drove up the West Side Highway, drinking coffee out of a Styrofoam cup and listening to Bruce Springsteen at top volume. It had been a long day.

Norman S. Rossinow. On September 11, he had been married for three months.

Nicholas P. Rossomando, firefighter, Rescue 5. **Michael Craig Rothberg. Donna Marie Rothenberg. Mark (Mickey) Rothenberg. James M. Roux. Nicholas Charles Alexander Rowe. Edward Veld Rowenhorst. Judy Rowlett. Sergeant Timothy Alan Roy Sr.,** police officer, NYPD. **Paul G. Ruback,** firefighter, Ladder 25.

Firehouse. The sleeping room was windowless. Arranged in two rows with an aisle between them, the single beds had iron frames that had been painted white a long time ago. On the ceiling there were fluorescent lights and exposed ductwork and plumbing. When unoccupied, the beds were neatly made with mismatched linens from home. There were some attempts at interior decoration: a scraggly plant in one corner, a threadbare throw rug on the green linoleum, a dusty gray gooseneck lamp on a red plastic milk crate. On the walls: a picture of young Elvis, a Yankees poster, a baseball schedule, a seascape in watercolors, a mountain scene in oils, a child's drawing of Godzilla, a wedding picture, a night photograph of the Manhattan skyline dominated by the Twin Towers and their ghostly reflections in the river below.

Ronald J. Ruben. Joanne Rubino. David Michael Ruddle. Bart Joseph Ruggiere. Susan Ann Ruggiero. Adam Keith Ruhalter. Gilbert Ruiz Sr.

Starting a family. Having now agreed that they were ready to have a baby, the couple found they both had strong feelings about breast-feeding versus bottle, day care versus a nanny, private school versus public, piano lessons versus violin. And the husband said he could already imagine what their son's bedroom would look like: sky-blue ceiling and grass-green carpet, walls painted with pictures of baseballs and bats and red squares for bases. What if it's a girl? his wife asked. No pink, he said, absolutely no pink, maybe a circus theme, or ballet. Do you think maybe, his wife mused, we've been watching too many home decorating shows lately?

Obdulio Ruiz-Diaz. Best friend of **Manuel John DaMota,** also killed.

Sergeant Major Robert E. Russell (retired). Stephen P. Russell, firefighter, Engine 55.

The sound of thunder bearing down on the city hard and fast from the west woke him in the middle of the night. He got up and opened the bedroom curtains so he could watch. He had always loved thunderstorms. He loved the look of the lightning searing straight down to the ground. He loved the tumult of the thunder, which at its climax sounded like gigantic square blocks colliding mere inches above his apartment building. He felt exhilarated, energized, and strangely hopeful, although he could not have said exactly what the storm made him hope for.

Steven Harris Russin. Expectant father. His twin daughters were born on September 15, 2001.

Lieutenant Michael Thomas Russo Sr., firefighter, Special Operations. **Wayne Alan Russo. Chief Warrant Officer William R. Ruth. Edward Ryan. John Joseph Ryan Jr.**

Retribution.

Jonathan Stephen Ryan. Expectant father. His second child, a boy, was born on October 15, 2001.

Kristin A. Irvine Ryan. On September 11, she had been married for three months.

Matthew Lancelot Ryan, firefighter, chief, Battalion 1. **Tatiana Ryjova. Christina Sunga Ryook.**

Revenge.

S

Thierry Saada. Expectant father. His first child, a boy, was born on October 21, 2001.

Jason Elazar Sabbag. Thomas E. Sabella, firefighter, Ladder 13. **Scott H. Saber. Charles E. Sabin Sr. Joseph Francis Sacerdote. Jessica Leigh Sachs. Francis John Sadocha. Jude Elias Safi.**

At 12:16 p.m. the FAA reports that American airspace has been cleared of all commercial and private aircraft. Only military jets remain in the air.

Brock Joel Safronoff. On September 11, he had been married for five weeks.

Edward Saiya. John Patrick Salamone. Marjorie C. Salamone. Hernando R. Salas. Juan G. Salas. Esmerlin Antonio Salcedo.

On Saturday afternoon they visited at least a dozen jewelry stores. By the end of the day their feet were sore and they were starting to get on each other's nerves. But then they found it: the perfect engagement ring. It was called Aphrodite, a half-carat round diamond in an eighteen-carat white-gold setting that spiraled delicately around the stone. It cost more than he had intended to spend, but she loved it so much. They placed the order and arranged the payment plan. The saleswoman said it would be ready in about two weeks.

John Salvatore Salerno Jr. Expectant father. His first child was due in March 2002.

Richard L. Salinardi Jr. Wayne John Saloman. Nolbert Salomon. Catherine Patricia Salter. Frank G. Salvaterra. Paul Richard Salvio. Samuel Robert Salvo Jr. Rena Sam-Dinnoo. Carlos Alberto Samaniego. John P. Sammartino. James Kenneth Samuel Jr. Michael V. San Phillip. Hugo M. Sanay-Perafiel. Alva Cynthia Jeffries Sanchez. Erick Sanchez.

The past. Fifteen years ago he suffered a fractured skull and lost two fingers in a car accident. Fifteen years ago, when he was fifteen, he and his three siblings were orphaned, and at the age of eighteen he became their legal guardian. Twelve years ago his older brother was killed while trying to land his fighter jet on an aircraft carrier. Eleven years ago, when he was thirteen, he almost died in a car accident. Ten years ago she spent six months in a body cast recovering from a spinal condition that could have left her a paraplegic. Ten years ago he recovered from a stroke that had destroyed his memory and left him paralyzed on the right side. Ten years ago his brother was killed in gang violence in their native Colombia. Ten years ago, when she was twenty-three, she was widowed, left to raise her two young daughters alone.

Jacquelyn Patrice Sanchez. September 17 was her son's first birthday.

Jesus Sanchez. Eric M. Sand. Stacy Leigh Sanders. Herman S. Sandler. James Sands Jr. Ayleen J. Santiago. Kirsten R. Santiago. Maria Theresa C. (Maritess) Santillan.

The future. She dreamed of having a big family, five children at least, maybe more. He dreamed of living on a farm with ducks, chickens, turkeys, and a couple of goats. She dreamed of living a life of simplicity and devotion to God. He dreamed of finally being able to bring his wife and children to America. She dreamed of graduating from college. He dreamed of attending a military academy. She dreamed of becoming a teacher. He dreamed of becoming a doctor. She dreamed of becoming a model. He dreamed of becoming a firefighter.

Susan Gayle Santo. Christopher Santora, firefighter, Engine 54. **John A. Santore,** firefighter, Ladder 5. **Mario L. Santoro,** emergency medical technician. **Rafael Humberto Santos. Rufino Conrado Flores (Roy) Santos. Captain Victor J. Saracini,** pilot, United Airlines Flight 175. **Kalyan K. Sarkar.**

The sound of thunder bearing down on the city hard and fast from the west woke her in the middle of the night. The dog had already crawled under the bed. She got up and unplugged the television, the computer, and all three phones. She had always been afraid of thunderstorms. She got back into bed and lay rigid in the dark as the lightning illuminated the room in heart-stopping white strokes she could see even through her clenched eyelids. By the time the storm passed, her nightgown was wet with sweat, her heart was jumping, and she was utterly exhausted. But still she could not get back to sleep.

Chapelle Renée Sarker. September 28 was her thirty-eighth birthday.

Paul F. Sarle. Expectant father. His third child, a boy, was born on February 28, 2002.

Deepika Kumar Sattaluri. Gregory Thomas Saucedo, firefighter, Ladder 5. **Susan M. Sauer. Anthony Savas. Vladimir Savinkin. John Michael Sbarbaro. Lieutenant Colonel David M. Scales. Robert Louis Scandole Jr. Michelle Scarpitta. Dennis Scauso,** firefighter, Haz-Mat 1.

On Monday evening she did six loads of laundry.

John Albert Schardt, firefighter, Engine 201. Expectant father. On September 12, his wife found out she was pregnant with their third child.

John G. Scharf. Frederick Claude Scheffold, firefighter, chief, Battalion 12. **Angela Susan Scheinberg. Scott Mitchell Schertzer. Sean Schielke. Steven Francis Schlag. Commander Robert Allan Schlegel. Jon S. Schlissel. Karen Helene Schmidt. Ian Schneider. Thomas G. Schoales,** firefighter, Engine 4. **Frank G. Schott Jr.**

Weather. She hated the wind, especially a hot wind from the west in August, which should have blown away the smog and the humidity but didn't, seeming instead to drive the bad air and the dirt more deeply into her skin, her nose, and her lungs. She hated the wind, especially a cold wind from the north in January, which rattled the windows and roared high up in the sky like a fleet of airplanes. She hated the wind because it filled her not with air but with a slurry of anxiety, a swampy farrago of impending doom.

Gerard Patrick Schrang, firefighter, Rescue 3. **Jeffrey H. Schreier. John T. Schroeder. Susan Lee Kennedy Schuler. Edward William Schunk. Mark E. Schurmeier. Clarin Shellie Siegel Schwartz. John Burkhart Schwartz.**

At 12:36 p.m., in a taped statement from Barksdale Air Force Base, President Bush assures the nation that those responsible for the attack will be hunted down and punished. He says, The resolve of our great nation is being tested. But make no mistake: we will show the world that we will pass this test.

He asks for prayers for the victims.

Mark Schwartz, emergency medical technician. September 19 was his twenty-fifth wedding anniversary.

Adriane Victoria Scibetta. Raphael (Ralph) Scorca. Janice M. Scott. Randolph Scott.

Recovered: the remains of three sculptures by Auguste Rodin. More than $7 million worth of fine art had been displayed in the offices of Cantor Fitzgerald, including drawings, casts, and nearly two dozen sculptures by Rodin, including *The Three Shades* and *The Thinker.*

Christopher Jay Scudder. Arthur Warren Scullin. Michael Herman Seaman. Margaret M. Seeliger. Anthony Segarra. Carlos Segarra. Jason M. Sekzer.

Just joking. When she took the job on the 94th floor, the young woman's family was worried. They kept talking about the terrorist bombing in 1993. She reminded them that she was now a single mother with three children to feed. It was a good job and she was lucky to have it. Still they pestered her. Her father said he couldn't sleep at night for thinking about her stuck way up there with no way to get out if something happened. She said, Don't worry, Dad. If the building is on fire, I'll jump.

Matthew Carmen Sellitto. September 30 was his twenty-fourth birthday.

Michael L. Selves. September 16 was his fifty-fourth birthday.

Howard Selwyn. Larry John Senko. Arturo Angelo Sereno.

On the desk. A coffee mug printed with Snoopy on his doghouse as the World War I Flying Ace. A clock with Santa Snoopy on the face. A pencil holder in the shape of Snoopy as a scarecrow. A bank in the shape of the Great Pumpkin. A mouse pad printed with the whole Peanuts gang. On the computer, a series of screensavers featuring Charlie Brown on the pitcher's mound, Schroeder at his piano, Lucy in the psychiatrist's booth, and Linus clutching his blanket. On the chair in the corner, a forty-eight-inch stuffed Snoopy wearing sunglasses and a red tie.

Frankie Serrano. September 23 was his twenty-fifth birthday.

Marian H. Serva. Alena Sesinova. Adele Christine Sessa. Sita Nermalla Sewnarine. Karen Lynn Seymour-Dietrich. Davis G. (Deeg) Sezna Jr. Thomas Joseph Sgroi. Jayesh S. Shah.

The things they were afraid of. Bumblebees. Lightning. Spiders. Thunder. Bats. Ladders. Horses. Clowns. Worms. Dentists. Dogs. Motorcycles. Lizards. Graveyards. Roller coasters. Centipedes. Needles. Snakes. Hospitals. Mimes. Bicycles. Cats. Guns. Mice. Doctors. Blood. Pain. The dark.

Khalid Mohammad Shahid. He was to be married in November 2001.

Mohammed Shajahan. Gary Shamay. Earl Richard Shanahan. Commander Dan Frederic Shanower.

Last seen wearing. Black pants, white shirt, black bow tie. Burgundy skirt, black blouse, multicolored Hermès scarf, black high heels. Loose white cotton pants and smock, large white chef's hat. Blue jeans, red T-shirt, denim Gap shirt, brown steel-toed boots. Black pants, black Gucci belt, black silk tank top, off-white see-through overshirt, gold strappy sandals. Dark blue work pants, light blue cotton work shirt with name embroidered in red above left breast pocket. Faded blue jeans, Hawaiian shirt, brown sandals. Copper-colored satin shirt, calf-length black suede skirt. Black Armani suit, white shirt with French collar and cuffs, onyx cuff links. Dark brown work pants, tan cotton work shirt, thick black belt with silver American eagle buckle.

Neil G. Shastri. On September 11, he had been married for three months.

Kathryn Anne Shatzoff. Barbara A. Shaw. Jeffrey James Shaw.

Post-it Notes. He would be the first to admit that he had an obsession. He had a whole collection of them: yellow, of course, and also hot pink, three shades of blue, mint green, lime green, purple, mauve, orange, and black (which could be written on only with gold or silver ink). Lined, unlined, small, medium, large, and extra-large (which were saved for special, longer missives). At work he stuck them all over his computer (and sometimes on other people's computers, too), reminders of one thing and another. At home he stuck them on the fridge *(Oops, I ate all the lunch meat),* in the fridge *(Who moved my cheese?),* on the calendar *(My birthday is in 200 days!),* in the dresser drawers *(These are my favorite socks: DO NOT BORROW),* and on his wife's pillow *(Good night, I love you).*

Robert John Shay Jr. Expectant father. His third child, a boy, was born on October 22, 2001.

Daniel James Shea. Joseph Patrick Shea. Brothers.

Robert Michael Shearer. Mary Kathleen Shearer. Husband and wife.

Linda J. Sheehan. Hagay Shefi. Antoinette (Toni) Sherman.

Police. He had once rescued more than a dozen children from an overturned school bus just before it burst into flames. He had overseen the logistics of security for events ranging from the U.S. Tennis Open to numerous presidential visits. In 1995 he went to Oklahoma City to help with the recovery efforts after the bombing of the Alfred P. Murrah Federal Building. He had once saved a young man who was threatening to jump from the roof of the Port Authority Bus Terminal. She had once saved her own mother's life, recognizing that her chest pains were due to blocked arteries. He had often been involved in recovering the bodies of people who had been pinned beneath subway trains: it was worse when they were still alive.

John Anthony Sherry. Brother-in-law of **Donald James McIntyre,** also killed.

Atsushi Shiratori. Thomas Joseph Shubert. Mark Shulman. See-Wong Shum. Allan Abraham Shwartzstein. Johanna Sigmund.

Salad maker. Salesman. Sanitary worker. Satellite communications engineer. Sculptor. Seamstress. Secretary. Security consultant. Security guard. Senior adviser on personnel issues to Joint Chiefs of Staff. Senior clinical adviser to U.S. Surgeon General. Sound engineer. Sous chef. Spiritual adviser. Staff writer. Stand-up comedian. Storekeeper. Store manager. Structural engineer. Subcontractor. Sunday school teacher. Supervisor. Supply manager. Switchboard operator. Systems support worker.

Dianne T. Signer. She was to be married on September 16, 2001. She was three months pregnant with her first child.

Gregory R. Sikorsky, firefighter, Squad 41. **Stephen Gerard Siller,** firefighter, Squad 1.

Firehouse. The record books were kept in the storeroom, hundreds of them, dating back to 1900, a detailed (if dusty) log of every alarm, every incident, every injury, and every fatality. From this mountain of paperwork the citywide yearly summary was distilled, a series of numbers in tables, a bloodless accounting of drama, misfortune, and disaster suffered or averted.

Calendar year 2000. Structural fires: 29,217. Nonstructural fires: 29,221. Malicious fire alarms: 56,283. Civilian fire fatalities: 125. Firefighter burns (requiring medical leave): 402.

Some of the men kept their own lifetime logbooks of the fires they had attended (too many), the people they had rescued (not enough), the babies they had delivered (the current record stood at five, with two being the same woman at different times).

David Silver. Expectant father. His second child, a girl, was born on October 9, 2001.

Craig A. Silverstein. Nasima Hameed Simjee. Bruce Edward Simmons. Donald Dean Simmons.

Grief. When her only child was killed in a car accident two days after her eighteenth birthday, the mother wished that she had died, too. Or instead. She had kissed her daughter good-bye that morning with no intuition at all of what was to come. She thought she would never recover. For months and months she was paralyzed by grief. Some days she could not get out of bed. Everything hurt: breathing, talking, thinking, walking, remembering, and forgetting. Nothing mattered. But then she did begin to recover, slowly, so slowly. She did not know exactly when it started or why. She still could not make sense of what had happened. But it had been ten years now, and finally she understood that the only lesson to be learned from such a loss was that everything mattered.

George W. Simmons. Diane M. Simmons. Husband and wife. They were traveling to Hawaii to spread her father's ashes beside her mother's.

Arthur Simon. Kenneth Alan Simon. Father and son. On September 11, Kenneth's first child, a girl, was four months old.

Michael John Simon. Paul Joseph Simon. Marianne Teresa Simone. Barry Simowitz. Jane Louise Simpkin.

Gifts. He had proposed to his wife on a cruise ship, and for their honeymoon he had surprised her with another cruise, this time to Tahiti. For their upcoming anniversary, he had bought her a new Volvo. There would also be the carefully orchestrated surprise delivery of a baby grand piano programmed to play their wedding song. After that he would whisk her away to London for the weekend. Even all of this, he thought, could not begin to express how much he loved her.

Jeff Lyal Simpson. He was the father of triplets.

Cheryle D. Sincock.

Distinguishing features. Left thumb reattached, right knee reconstructed. Eighty percent blind. Scar from his back around the left side to the middle of his chest, eight-inch scar on left shin, fresh stitches mark on his chin. Surgical incision on her left breast. Six feet, ten inches tall. Pierced tongue. Partially deaf as a result of the 1993 bombing. Three-inch scar on the back of his head, semicircle scar from left armpit to the center of his chest (cancer fifteen years ago). Four-inch round strawberry birthmark on her left buttock. Two front teeth bonded, right tooth slightly discolored. Scar from her back to her stomach on left side (kidney removed). Scar on right side of his head (brain surgery). Black mole on her left shoulder, pinky toe overlapped by next toe on both feet, violet-red polish on fingernails. Both breasts removed.

Khamladai K. (Khami) Singh. Roshan Ramesh (Sean) Singh. Sister and brother.

Thomas Edison Sinton III.

Sacred.

Peter A. Siracuse. On September 11, his first child, a boy, was almost seven months old.

Muriel Fay Siskopoulos. Joseph Michael Sisolak. John P. Skala, police officer, Port Authority. **Francis Joseph Skidmore Jr. Toyena Corliss Skinner. Paul Albert Skrzypek. Christopher Paul Slattery. Vincent Robert Slavin. Robert F. Sliwak. Paul K. Sloan.**

Searching.

Stanley S. Smagala Jr., firefighter, Engine 226. Expectant father. His first child, a girl, was born on January 9, 2002.

Wendy L. Small. Technician Gregg Harold Smallwood.

Recovered: the remains of two public sculptures, Alexander Calder's *World Trade Center Stabile* and Fritz Koenig's *Sphere for Plaza Fountain.* Ripped open and filled with debris from the falling towers, *Sphere* was later cleaned and reinstalled in Battery Park. On March 11, 2002, the six-month anniversary of the attacks, it was dedicated in its damaged state as a memorial to the victims.

Catherine T. Smith. Daniel Laurence Smith. Lieutenant Colonel Gary F. Smith (retired). George Eric Smith. Heather Lee Smith. James Gregory Smith. Jeffrey Randall Smith. Joyce Patricia Smith. Karl Trumbull Smith.

Former lives. As a child he had lived in a clay hut in Africa. Through a combination of his own determination and a few lucky breaks, he had made his way to culinary school in France. And now here he was: a pastry chef at Windows on the World. Sometimes he could hardly believe it himself: how much his life had changed, how much *he* had changed, how much he had to be grateful for every single day.

Kevin Joseph Smith, firefighter, Haz-Mat 1. He was the father of eight children.

Leon Smith Jr., firefighter, Ladder 118.

In the dream, which occurred three times in August, a young man was walking down an empty hospital corridor searching for someone. There was no sound and everything was silver and white. There were bright lights in the ceiling. It was cold. There were no doctors, no nurses, and no patients in any of the empty rooms.

Moira Ann Reddy Smith, police officer. She was the only female member of the NYPD to die on September 11.

Rosemary A. Smith. Sandra Fajardo Smith. Bonnie Jeanne Smithwick. Rochelle Monique Snell.

At 1:15 p.m. President Bush reboards Air Force One and heads for Offutt Air Force Base, near Omaha, Nebraska.

Christine Anne Snyder. On September 11, she had been married for three months.

Dianne Bullis Snyder, flight attendant, American Airlines Flight 11. **Leonard Joseph Snyder Jr. Astrid Elizabeth Sohan. Sushil S. Solanki. Ruben Solares. Naomi Leah Solomon. Daniel W. Song. Mari-Rae Sopper. Michael Charles Sorresse. Fabian Soto.**

Lucky. The executive assistant considered herself lucky to be alive. After two surgeries and months of chemotherapy and radiation, the cancer was gone. Her hair was growing back, she had returned to work part-time, and now even a bad day felt like a blessing.

Timothy Patrick Soulas. Expectant father. His sixth child, a boy, was born on March 30, 2002.

Gregory T. Spagnoletti. Donald F. Spampinato Jr.

Shiva.

Thomas Sparacio. Expectant father. His wife was pregnant with their third child. The baby was stillborn on March 16, 2002.

John Anthony Spataro.

The things they loved. He loved making wine. She loved baking bread. He loved watching the History Channel. She loved parties, whether with bankers or bikers, it didn't matter. He loved late romantic dinners by candelight. She loved playing backgammon. He loved playing dominoes. She loved the smell of the ocean. He loved Dr. Seuss. She loved Japanese films. He loved the Seattle Mariners. She loved the Toronto Blue Jays. He loved the Minnesota Vikings. She loved the Colorado Avalanche. He loved the Detroit Lions. She loved tap dancing. He loved going to Disney World, with or without the kids. She loved staying in her pajamas all day on Sunday. He loved vacuuming to relieve stress. She loved Irish music. He loved karaoke. She loved U2. He loved Billy Joel. She loved Gloria Estefan. He loved Joe Cocker. She loved Andrea Bocelli.

Robert W. Spear Jr., firefighter, Engine 50. Brother-in-law of **Timothy Aaron Haviland,** also killed.

Robert Speisman. Maynard S. Spence Jr. George Edward Spencer III.

The things they hated. She hated having to ask for help. He hated having to ask for directions. She hated having to miss church. He hated talking on the phone. She hated being sick, even for one day. He hated wearing an overcoat, even when it snowed. She hated sitting around doing nothing. He hated gossip. She hated exercise. He hated being the center of attention. She hated saying no to anybody. He hated losing. She hated e-mail. He hated cell phones. She hated her crooked nose. He hated fancy restaurants. She hated not having enough money to buy her children everything they wanted. He hated the thought of retiring. She hated being so busy all the time. He hated speaking in public. She hated her son's blue hair. He hated his daughter's boyfriend's nose ring and tongue stud. She hated being so tall. He hated being so short. She hated rap music. He hated jazz.

Robert Andrew Spencer. On September 11, his third child, a boy, was twenty-seven days old.

Mary Rubina Sperando. Frank J. Spinelli, volunteer emergency medical technician. **William E. Spitz. Joseph P. Spor Jr.,** firefighter, Ladder 38. **Klaus Johannes Sprockcamp. Saranya Srinuan.**

At 1:27 p.m. a state of emergency is declared in Washington, D.C.

Fitzroy St. Rose. Michael F. Stabile. Lawrence T. Stack, firefighter, chief, Battalion 50. **Captain Timothy Stackpole,** firefighter, Division 11. **Richard James Stadelberger. Eric Adam Stahlman. Gregory M. Stajk,** firefighter, Ladder 13.

Favorite books. *The English Patient* by Michael Ondaatje. *Love Is a Dog from Hell* by Charles Bukowski. *Jewels of the Sun* by Nora Roberts. *The Unicorn Hunt* by Dorothy Dunnett. *Testimonies* by Patrick O'Brian. *Lathe of Heaven* by Ursula K. Le Guin. *Odds Against* by Dick Francis. *Fear and Loathing in Las Vegas* by Hunter S. Thompson. *The Tommyknockers* by Stephen King. *Cryptonomicon* by Neal Stephenson. *New Market Wizards: Conversations with America's Top Traders* by Jack D. Schwager.

Alexandru Liviu Stan. Corina Stan. Husband and wife.

Mary Domenica Stanley. Anthony M. Starita. Jeffrey Stark, firefighter, Engine 230.

Relief. Every time he came home from work safely, his wife said a quick silent prayer of thanks and buried her face in his neck with relief, inhaling the smoke from his hair and his skin. She knew it would never be easy being married to a firefighter, but she had to admit she'd grown to love that smell and the feel of his sweat against her cheek.

Derek James Statkevicus. Expectant father. His second child, a boy, was born on January 2, 2002.

Patricia J. Statz.

Family man. When he wasn't outside teaching his son to ride his bike without the training wheels, he was in the garage workshop building a rocking horse and a dollhouse for his daughter. When they discovered his wife was pregnant again, he immediately set to work building a wooden cradle just like the one his own mother had been rocked in when she was a baby. When the cradle was finished, he thought he would try his hand at making a high chair, a much more complicated project, but he thought he could do it.

Craig William Staub. Expectant father. His first child, a girl, was born on September 22, 2001, his thirty-first birthday.

William V. Steckman. Eric Thomas Steen. William R. Steiner. Alexander Robbins Steinman. Edna Lee Stephens. Andrew Stergiopoulos. Andrew Stern. Norma Lang Steuerle. Martha Stevens. Michael James Stewart. Richard H. Stewart Jr. Sanford M. Stoller. Douglas Joel Stone. Lonny Jay Stone. Jimmy Nevill Storey. Timothy C. Stout.

Distinguishing features: tattoos. Baby tiger's face on her lower back, Japanese character for man/husband and the name *Louie* on her right pelvic bone. College fraternity symbol on his left hip. Nickname *Grumpy* on his right calf. British Lions on both shoulder blades, a gryphon on her chest. *UCLA Bruin* on his left thigh, green four-leaf clover on his right arm. Nickname *Yosemite Sam* on his left shoulder. Black fish on his right arm. Large American flag and *USMC* (United States Marine Corps) on his right arm.

Thomas S. Strada. On September 11, his third child, a boy, was four days old.

James J. Straine Jr. On September 11, his second child, a boy, was one week old.

Edward William Straub. George J. Strauch Jr. Edward T. Strauss. Steven R. Strauss.

The things they carried. Cream-colored padded canvas bag containing six rolls of film and three cameras. Two clear blue glass marbles and a ball of string in pants pocket. Green and white diaper bag containing a brown and orange stuffed tiger and a yellow sundress, size two. Small Phillips screwdriver with blue plastic handle. Brown suede briefcase containing wallpaper samples, paint chips, 2002 opera schedule, and a pitchpipe. Large black tote bag printed on both sides with the Manhattan skyline at night beneath a full moon, containing travel guide to New York City and six postcards of the Statue of Liberty.

Sergeant Major Larry L. Strickland. He was to retire in one month after thirty years of army service.

Steven Frank Strobert.

Labor Day barbecue. Cars filled the driveway and spilled onto the street in front of the house. Everyone brought food and something to drink. Everyone also brought their children and their dogs. Attracted by the hubbub and the smell of meat cooking, the neighbors came over, too. The men had a contest to see who could make the biggest splash in the pool. One by one they cannonballed off the diving board until everyone was soaked and both the dogs and the children were barking hysterically. Then they ate too much and played badminton to work it off. Much later the few remaining adults sat around in lawn chairs, batting away moths and mosquitoes, counting the stars, and jiggling the ice in their glasses in the dark.

Walwyn W. Stuart Jr., police officer, Port Authority. September 28 was his daughter's first birthday.

Benjamin Suarez, firefighter, Ladder 21. **David Scott Suarez. Ramon Saurez,** police officer, NYPD. **Xavier Suarez.**

At 1:44 p.m. the Pentagon announces that five warships and two aircraft carriers will depart the Norfolk Naval Station in Virginia, to protect the eastern seaboard from possible further attack.

Yoichi Sugiyama. William Christopher Sugra. Daniel Suhr, firefighter, Engine 216. **David Marc Sullins,** paramedic.

What remains. Ten Bruce Springsteen posters. Nine high-school basketball trophies. Eight custom-made guitars. Seven needlepoint pictures of lighthouses. Six talking parrots. Five bottles of Stetson cologne. Four lawn-and-leaf bags containing thirty years' worth of bank deposit and withdrawal slips, credit card receipts, and income tax returns. Three electric train sets. Three miniature towns named after his daughters. Three glass jars of steel pennies from the World War II era, when copper was in short supply. Two crystal goblets in the Happiness pattern from Waterford's Millennium Collection. Two rocks from a mountaintop in Ireland.

Lieutenant Christopher P. Sullivan, firefighter, Ladder 111. **Patrick Sullivan.**

Silence.

Thomas G. Sullivan. Brother-in-law of **Lawrence Patrick Dickinson,** also killed.

Hilario Soriano (Larry) Sumaya. James Joseph Suozzo. Colleen M. Supinski.

Strength.

Robert Sutcliffe Jr. Expectant father. His twin boys were born on January 16, 2002.

Selina Sutter. Claudia Suzette Sutton.

Secrets. Of course his wife knew he was a window washer, but for years she thought he only washed the windows on the *inside.* He did nothing to correct this misconception. What good would it do to tell her that he actually operated the machines that inched up and down the outside of the towers? She would just worry herself sick. What good would it do to tell her that several times a year he and his partner went up and manually washed the highest windows that the machines couldn't do? She wouldn't let him go to work if she knew. She would never believe that he was perfectly safe up there, harnessed into his little dangling bucket thirteen hundred feet above the street. He had no sense of fear and he knew she would never understand how much he loved it.

John Francis Swaine. Brother-in-law of **John Armand Reo,** also killed.

Kristine M. Swearson. Brian David Sweeney. Brian Edward Sweeney, firefighter, Rescue 1. **Madeline (Amy) Sweeney,** flight attendant, American Airlines Flight 11. **Kenneth J. Swenson.Thomas F. Swift.**

On Saturday afternoon he liked nothing better than to take a trip to Home Depot. Sometimes his wife went with him, but in truth he preferred to go alone because she always got impatient, sharing neither his devotion to the religion of DIY nor his enthusiasm for every single offering in this vast temple of home improvement. Alone, he could spend all afternoon studying the plumbing fixtures, the paintbrushes, the spools of copper wire, the brass and glass doorknobs, the ceramic tiles, and the weather-stripping. He fairly genuflected in front of the power tools and often came home with something he hadn't known he needed (a palm sander, a miter box, a staple gun, a laser level, a jigsaw) but was now absolutely certain he could not live without.

Derek Ogilvie Sword. He became engaged on August 25, 2001.

Kevin Thomas Szocik. On September 11, he had been married for four months.

Gina Sztejnberg.

Military honors. Southwest Asia Service Medal. Navy and Marine Corps Commendation Medal. Joint Service Achievement Medal. Kuwait Liberation Medal. Navy Expeditionary Medal. Armed Forces Service Medal. NATO Medal. Antarctic Service Medal. Navy "E" Ribbon. Defense Superior Service Award. Joint Services Commendation Medal. Navy and Marine Corps Overseas Service Ribbon. Coast Guard Meritorious Unit Commendation. Rifle Marksmanship Medal. Pistol Marksmanship Medal. Sailor of the Year.

Norbert P. Szurkowski. Expectant father. His second child was due in May 2002.

T

Harry Taback. Joann Tabeek. Norma C. Taddei. Michael Taddonio. Keiichiro Takahashi. Keiji Takahashi. Phyllis Gail Talbot. Robert R. Talhami.

What remains. One man-sized chicken costume with yellow-feathered body; yellow rubber feet and beak; red rubber gloves, wings, and crop.

John Talignani. He was flying to San Francisco to claim the body of his stepson, who was killed in a car accident there while on his honeymoon.

Sean Patrick Tallon, firefighter, Ladder 10.

Last seen wearing. Engagement ring with wide platinum band and oval diamond, gold chain with diamond cross. Gold puzzle ring on her left ring finger, silver cross with amethyst stone on silver chain. Superman ring. Winnie-the-Pooh watch on her left wrist, XOXO bracelet on right. Two gold bracelets on his right wrist, watch with black band on left, diamond stud in his left earlobe, tricolor gold ring with three interlocking bands on left ring finger, small silver ring on right. Silver chain with eagle, small mezuzah case, miniature drumstick, pictures of his children, and the letter *F* cast in solid silver.

Paul Talty, police officer, NYPD. On September 11, his third child, a girl, was one month old.

Maurita Tam. Niece of **Wai-ching Chung,** also killed.

Rachel Tamares. Hector Tamayo. Michael Andrew Tamuccio. Kenichiro Tanaka. Rhondelle Cherie Tankard. Michael Anthony Tanner.

The future. She dreamed of visiting fifty different countries by the time she turned fifty. He dreamed of making his first million dollars by the time he turned thirty. She dreamed of losing twenty pounds before her wedding in the spring. He dreamed of meeting the President and the First Lady. She dreamed of marrying her lover if he ever left his wife. He dreamed of traveling across the country to visit famous baseball fields. She dreamed of climbing Mount Everest. He dreamed of returning to his homeland with enough money to buy his own cockfighting ring.

Dennis Gerard Taormina Jr. September 7 was his tenth wedding anniversary.

Kenneth Joseph Tarantino. Expectant father. His second child, a boy, was born on December 7, 2001, his wife's birthday.

Allan Tarasiewicz, firefighter, Rescue 5. September 12 was his wife's birthday.

Michael C. (Mac) Tarrou, flight attendant, United Airlines Flight 175. Boyfriend of **Amy R. King,** flight attendant, United Airlines Flight 175, also killed.

Ronald Tartaro. Darryl Anthony Taylor. Donnie Brooks Taylor. Hilda E. Taylor.

Tax accountant. Tax auditor. Tax investigator. Taxi driver. Teacher. Telephone technician. Television cameraman. Temporary employee. Tourist. Trader. Transmitter engineer. Transportation designer. Travel agent.

Major Kip P. Taylor, posthumously promoted to lieutenant colonel. Expectant father. His second child, a boy, was born on October 25, 2001.

Leonard E. Taylor.

At 2:50 p.m. President Bush arrives at Offutt Air Force Base in Nebraska, the headquarters of the U.S. Strategic Command, which controls the American nuclear arsenal. There he enters a cinder-block bunker, from which he communicates with the National Security Council in Washington by telephone.

Lorisa Ceylon Taylor. September 10 was her seventh wedding anniversary.

Michael Morgan Taylor. Sandra Carol Taylor. Sandra D. Teague. Karl W. Teepe. Paul A. Tegtmeier, firefighter, Engine 4. **Yeshavant Moreshwar Tembe.**

Tears.

Anthony Tempesta. September 11 was his daughter's seventh birthday.

Dorothy Pearl Temple. Stanley L. Temple. David Tengelin.

English as a second language. The sous chef was taking a course two nights a week. They were learning the names of the parts of the body. In the workbook there were diagrams with numbers on each part and then the matching words below: *brain, lung, heart, liver, stomach, kidney, muscle, bone, skull, skin.* The teacher had told them that next week they were going on to the unit called Feelings. This included drawings of people in different situations with many different expressions on their faces. There were so many words: *calm, nervous, disgusted, worried, relieved, lonely, sad, homesick, proud, scared, embarrassed, excited, angry, bored, confused, happy, surprised, in love.* How would he ever be able to remember them all? It was hard enough to understand what other people were feeling in his own language, let alone trying to figure it out in English, too.

Brian John Terrenzi. Expectant father. His first child, a girl, was born on December 9, 2001.

Lisa Marie Terry. Goumatie T. Thackurdeen. Harshad Sham Thatte.

On Monday evening they made love. Twice.

Michael Theodoridis. Rahma Salie Theodoridis. Husband and wife. Rahma was seven months pregnant with their first child.

Thomas Francis Theurkauf Jr. Early in 2001 he was named top banking analyst in the United States by the *Wall Street Journal.*

Lesley Anne Thomas-O'Keefe. Brian Thomas Thompson. Clive (Ian) Thompson. Glenn Thompson. Nigel Bruce Thompson. Perry Anthony Thompson. Vanavah Alexei Thompson. Captain William Harry Thompson.

The past. Ten years ago her eighteen-year-old daughter was killed in a car accident. Nine years ago her twenty-six-year-old son died of a brain aneurysm. Seven years ago his brother died after three years in a coma caused by a fall. Seven years ago one of her six children died of AIDS contracted from a blood transfusion. Two years ago his brother died of a congenital heart problem. Two years ago his home was completely destroyed by fire. One year ago he went into a coma after being knocked unconscious by the flying boom of a catamaran. Five months ago his fifteen-year-old daughter died of a brain tumor despite twenty-one operations. Four months ago he had a near-death experience during surgery for a herniated disk in his neck.

Eric Raymond Thorpe. Nichola Angela Thorpe. Sergeant Tamara C. Thurman. Sal Edward Tieri Jr.

The things they loved. She loved skydiving. He loved playing paintball. She loved British comedies. He loved war movies. She loved entertaining. He loved Broadway shows. She loved playing the piano. He loved driving fast. She loved bargain hunting at the outlet mall. He loved playing chess. She loved visiting the Sistine Chapel. He loved running with the bulls in Pamplona. She loved growing roses. He loved reading newspapers, usually five a day. She loved building sandcastles with her sons. He loved playing Go Fish with his daughters. She loved going to the zoo. He loved washing his new car. She loved getting to work in time to see the sunrise. He loved the smell of sawdust. She loved the smell of apples. He loved meeting new people and had learned to ask "Do you like Chinese food?" in seventeen languages because it was a good conversation starter.

John Patrick Tierney, firefighter, Ladder 9. He had been on the job for six weeks.

Mary Ellen Tiesi. William Randolph Tieste. Kenneth Francis Tietjen, police officer, Port Authority.

For better, for worse. For richer, for poorer. In sickness and in health. During the thirty years of their marriage, his wife had suffered from a variety of debilitating conditions, including diabetes, thyroid disease, chronic pancreatitis, high blood pressure, and high cholesterol. With quiet and unwavering devotion, he took care of her and he prayed. Several times he tried to brace himself for losing her, but she was a survivor: always she had rallied and pulled through. Never once had it occurred to either of them that he could be the one to die first.

Stephen Edward Tighe. Brother-in-law of **Timothy Michael O'Brien,** also killed.

Scott Charles Timmes. Michael E. Tinley. Jennifer Marie Tino. Robert Frank Tipaldi. John James Tipping II, firefighter, Ladder 4.

What remains. One Ping-Pong table painted blue and silver, the colors of the Dallas Cowboys. One pair of gorilla slippers, men's size twelve. One scale model of Ebbets Field. One five-foot-long boa constrictor named Pumpkin.

David Lawrence Tirado. Hector Luis Tirado Jr., firefighter, Engine 23. **Michelle Lee Titolo. Alicia Nicole Titus,** flight attendant, United Airlines Flight 175. **John J. Tobin. Richard J. Todisco. Lieutenant Commander Otis Vincent Tolbert. Vladimir Tomasevic. Stephen Kevin Tompsett. Thomas Tong. Doris S. Torres.**

Tenderness.

Luis Eduardo Torres. Expectant father. His third child, a boy, was born on October 31, 2001.

Amy Elizabeth Toyen. Christopher Michael Traina. Daniel Patrick Trant. Abdoul Karim Traoré. Glenn J. Travers. Walter Philip Travers. Felicia Yvette Traylor-Bass.

In the photo album. The towers in the morning viewed from the harbor with the Statue of Liberty in the foreground. The towers in the afternoon viewed from the plaza, looking up through the stainless steel sculpture called *Ideogram* by James Rosati. The towers viewed close up with the bell tower of Saint Nicholas Greek Orthodox Church in the foreground. The towers at dusk viewed from the street, looking up through a low cover of clouds. The towers silhouetted against an orange sky with the sun setting between them. The towers at night on the Fourth of July with fireworks bursting on the water.

James Anthony Trentini. Mary Barbara Trentini. Husband and wife.

Lisa L. Spina Trerotola.

Last wishes. He wanted his family and friends to have a big party at Nobu, his favorite sushi restaurant. She wanted her ashes to be scattered off the Na Pali cost of Kauai. He wanted "Amazing Grace" to be played at his funeral, followed by a selection of his favorite Grateful Dead songs. She wanted her ashes to be dug into the ground and an apple tree planted there. He wanted his eulogy to be delivered in four languages to honor his multicultural heritage. She wanted no flowers. He wanted no singing. She wanted to be buried in the rain.

Karamo Trerra. September 12 was his fourth wedding anniversary.

Michael Angel Trinidad. Francis Joseph Trombino. Gregory James Trost. Willie Quincy Troy.

Testament.

William P. Tselepis Jr. Expectant father. His second child, a boy, was born on October 5, 2001.

Zhanetta Valentinovna Tsoy. On August 23, 2001, she arrived in the United States for the first time, having emigrated from Kazakhstan. September 11 was her first day of work in America.

Michael Patrick Tucker. Pauline Tull-Francis.

At 4:00 p.m. officials announce that there are credible indications that Osama bin Laden is responsible for the attacks.

Lance Richard Tumulty. On September 11, his second child, a girl, was four months old.

Ching Ping Tung.

The collective weight of the passengers aboard United Airlines Flight 93, which crashed in Pennsylvania, was estimated at 7,500 pounds by the coroner. Only 600 pounds of human remains were recovered from the crash site. The plane was also carrying thousands of pounds of mail destined for California. Envelopes and magazines covered the ground and hung from the trees. Some pieces were burned while others were recovered still in perfect condition. Debris was found up to eight miles from the point of impact.

Simon James Turner. Expectant father. His first child, a boy, was born on November 14, 2001.

Donald Joseph Tuzio. Robert T. Twomey. Jennifer Lynn Tzemis.

Devotion. *Hail Mary, full of grace.* Early each morning she went into Saint Nicholas Greek Orthodox Church, across the street from the South Tower, where she worked. *The Lord is with thee.* The church was tiny, only thirty-five feet high, but in it there were icons from the Russian czar Nicholas II and holy relics of Saint Catherine of Siena (patron saint of nurses, philosophy, and spinsters; invoked against fire) and Saint Nicholas himself (patron saint of bakers, barrel makers, bootblacks, brewers, brides, children, dockworkers, fishermen, Greece, merchants, pawnbrokers, perfumers, prisoners, sailors, and travelers). *Blessed art thou among women, and blessed is the fruit of thy womb, Jesus.* Each morning she said the Rosary and prayed to the Virgin. *Holy Mary, Mother of God, pray for us sinners, now and at the hour of our death.* Each morning she was comforted. *Amen.*

U

John G. Ueltzhoffer. Tyler V. Ugolyn.

Unthinkable.

Michael A. Uliano. Best friend of **Andrew Anthony Abate** and **Vincent P. Abate,** also killed. September 2 was his forty-second birthday.

Jonathan J. Uman. Anil Shivhari Umarkar.

Unspeakable.

Allen V. Upton.

Unbearable.

Diane Marie Urban. Best friend of **Dianne Gladstone,** also killed.

V

John Damien Vaccacio. Bradley Hodges Vadas. William Valcarel. Mayra Valdes-Rodriguez.

Devotion. Each day he studied the Koran. *In the Name of God, the Beneficent, the Merciful. Praise be to God, Lord of the Worlds, the Beneficent, the Merciful. Owner of the Day of Judgment, Thee alone we worship; Thee alone we ask for help.* Each day he prayed five times at the prescribed hours, no matter where he was. Even at work he stopped whatever he was doing and prayed facing Mecca, on his knees with his head bowed down to the floor. *I bear witness that there is none worthy of being worshipped except God. I bear witness that Muhammad is the Messenger of God. Come to Prayer. Come to Success.* Each day these prayers defined his life more distinctly than any clock or calendar ever could. *He is God, the One—God, the eternally besought of all. He begets not, nor is He begotten. And there is none comparable unto him.* Each day he was comforted. *There is no God but Allah.*

Felix Antonio Vale. Ivan Vale. Brothers.

Benito Valentin. Santos Valentin Jr., police officer, NYPD. **Carlton Francis Valvo. Pendyala Vamshikrishna. Erica H. Van Acker. Kenneth W. Van Auken. Richard Bruce Van Hine,** firefighter, Squad 41. **Daniel M. Van Laere.**

What remains. One small blue blowtorch used to make crème brûlée.

Edward Raymond Vanacore. Jon C. Vandevander. Frederick Thomas Varacchi. Gopalakrishnan (Gopal) Varadhan. David Vargas. Scott C. Vasel. Azael Ismael Vasquez. Santos Vasquez.

Valor.

Lieutenant Commander Ronald James Vauk. Expectant father. His second child, a girl, was born on November 1, 2001.

Arcangel Vazquez. Peter Anthony Vega, firefighter, Ladder 118. **Sankara S. Velamuri. Jorge Velazquez. Lawrence G. Veling,** firefighter, Engine 235. **Anthony Mark Ventura. David Vera. Loretta Ann Vero. Christopher James Vialonga. Matthew Gilbert Vianna.**

Vanished.

Robert Anthony Vicario. On September 11, his first child, a girl, was three months old.

Celeste Torres Victoria. Joanna Vidal.

Ventilation engineer. Vertical transportation manager. Vice president. Video technician. Volume control clerk.

John T. Vigiano II, firefighter, Ladder 132. **Joseph Vincent Vigiano,** detective, NYPD. Brothers. On September 11, Joseph's third child, a boy, was three months old.

Frank J. Vignola Jr. Joseph Barry Vilardo. Sergio Villanueva, firefighter, Ladder 132. **Chantal Vincelli. Melissa Renée Vincent. Francine Ann Virgilio. Lawrence Joseph Virgilio,** firefighter, Squad 18.

At 4:10 p.m. Building 7 of the World Trade Center complex is burning.

Joseph Gerard Visciano. Joshua S. Vitale. Maria Percoco Vola. Lynette D. Vosges. Garo H. Voskerijian. Alfred Vukosa.

What remains. One souped-up white Mustang with flashing lights, an ambulance siren, and a bumper sticker that reads *No Fear.*

W

Gregory Kamal Bruno Wachtler. Lieutenant Colonel Karen J. Wagner.

Waiter. Wallpaper hanger. Watch commander. Wedding singer. Window washer. Wire person. Women's gymnastic coach. Writer.

Mary Alice Wahlstrom. Mother of **Carolyn Beug,** also killed.

Honor Elizabeth Wainio. Gabriela S. Waisman. Wendy Alice Rosario Wakeford. Courtney Wainsworth Walcott. Victor Wald. Kenneth E. Waldie. Benjamin James Walker. Glen James Wall.

Waiting.

Mitchel Scott Wallace, emergency medical technician. **Peter Guyder Wallace. Lieutenant Robert Francis Wallace,** firefighter, Engine 205. **Roy Michael Wallace.**

Weeping.

Jeanmarie Wallendorf. Matthew Blake Wallens. Meta L. Fuller Waller. John Wallice Jr. Barbara P. Walsh.

Whisper.

James Henry Walsh. September 11 was his daughter's second birthday.

Jeffrey Patrick Walz, firefighter, Ladder 9; posthumously promoted to lieutenant. **Ching Huei Wang. Weibin Wang. Lieutenant Michael Warchola,** firefighter, Ladder 5. **Stephen Gordon Ward. Timothy Ray Ward. James Arthur Waring.**

Witness.

Brian Warner. On September 11, his second child, a girl, was two months old.

Derrick Christopher Washington. Charles Waters. James Thomas (Muddy) Waters Jr. Captain Patrick J. Waters, firefighter, Special Operations.

What remains. One pair of orange Converse sneakers painted with black tiger stripes, the colors of the Cincinnati Bengals.

Kenneth Thomas Watson, firefighter, Engine 214. **Michael Henry Waye. Todd Christopher Weaver. Walter Edward Weaver,** police officer, NYPD. **Nathaniel Webb,** police officer, Port Authority.

At 4:36 p.m. President Bush boards Air Force One and leaves Offutt Air Force Base in Nebraska, en route to Washington, D.C.

Dinah Webster. Fiancée of **Neil James Cudmore,** also killed.

William Michael Weems. Joanne Flora Weil. Michael T. Weinberg, firefighter, Engine 1. **Steven Jay Weinberg.**

What remains. One battered prayer card with a book of matches stapled to it, a good luck charm inadvertently left at home on Tuesday morning.

Scott Jeffrey Weingard. September 23 was his thirtieth birthday.

Steven George Weinstein. Simon V. Weiser. David Martin Weiss, firefighter, Rescue 1. **David Thomas Weiss. Specialist Chin Sun Pak Wells.**

At 5:20:33 p.m. the 47-story World Trade Center Building 7 collapses. The seismograph station at Palisades, New York, 21 miles north of Lower Manhattan, operated by the Lamont-Doherty Earth Observatory of Columbia University, registers the seismic equivalent of the collapse at 0.6 on the Richter scale for a duration of 18 seconds.

Vincent Michael Wells. September 17 was his twenty-third birthday.

Deborah Anne Jacobs Welsh, flight attendant, United Airlines Flight 93. **Timothy Matthew Welty,** firefighter, Squad 288. **Christian Hans Rudolf Wemmers. Ssu-Hui (Vanessa) Wen. John Joseph Wenckus.**

What remains. One pair of Gucci boots, size seven, green with gold trim, still in the box, wrapped in tissue paper, unworn.

Oleh D. Wengerchuk. September 27 was his thirty-second wedding anniversary.

Peter Matthew West. Whitfield West Jr. Meredith Lynn Whalen. Eugene Whelan, firefighter, Engine 230.

The fires at Ground Zero will continue to burn for more than three months. They will be officially declared extinguished on December 20, with a warning that some small fires might still be burning beneath the rubble and could be reignited by the removal of more debris.

Adam S. White. Edward James White III, firefighter, Engine 230. **James Patrick White. John Sylvester White. Kenneth Wilburn White Jr. Leonard Anthony White. Malissa Y. White. Staff Sergeant Maudlyn Alberta White. Kristin Gould White. Sandra Letitia White. Wayne White.**

Lost.

Firefighters: 343.

NYPD officers: 23.

Port Authority police officers: 37, the largest single-day loss suffered by any American police force in history.

Leanne Marie Whiteside. Mark P. Whitford, firefighter, Engine 23. **Michael T. Wholey,** police officer, Port Authority. **Mary Catherine Lenz Wieman. Jeffrey David Wiener.**

Before September 11, the number of firefighters who had died in the line of duty in the entire 136-year history of the FDNY was 752. Before September 11, the highest number of FDNY firefighters who had died in a single day at a single fire was 12.

William Joseph Wik. Alison Marie Wildman. Lieutenant Glenn E. Wilkinson, firefighter, Engine 238. **Ernest M. Willcher. John Charles Willett.**

More than 250 search and rescue dogs worked in the recovery efforts at Ground Zero and the Pentagon. This number included Labrador and golden retrievers, German shepherds, collies, rottweilers, and scores of mixed-breed dogs.

Brian Patrick Williams. Candace Lee Williams. Crossley Richard Williams Jr. David J. Williams. Lieutenant Commander David Lucian Williams. Deborah Lynn Williams. Major Dwayne Williams.

There are 221 firehouses in the five boroughs of New York City. On September 11, more than 70 of those houses lost members, and 91 fire trucks were buried beneath the rubble.

Kevin Michael Williams. He was to be married in December 2001.

Louie Anthony Williams. Louis Calvin Williams III. Lieutenant John P. Williamson, firefighter, chief, Battalion 6. **Donna Ann Wilson. William Eben Wilson.**

Each of the twenty-three NYPD officers who died on September 11 was posthumously awarded the Congressional Medal of Honor.

David Harold Winton. He was to be married on November 17, 2001.

Glenn J. Winuk. Thomas Francis Wise. Alan L. Wisniewski. Frank Thomas (Paul) Wisniewski. David Wiswall. Sigrid Charlotte Wiswe.

Lost.

World Trade Center: 2,749.

Pentagon: 184.

Pennsylvania: 40.

Total: 2,973.

Each death was declared a homicide in the official medical records.

Michael Robert Wittenstein. He was to be married on October 20, 2001.

Christopher W. Wodenshek. September 22 was his thirty-sixth birthday.

Martin P. Wohlforth. September 13 was his twenty-first wedding anniversary.

Katherine Susan Wolf. Jennifer Yen Wong. Jenny Seu Kueng Low Wong. Siu Cheung (Steve) Wong. Yin Ping (Steven) Wong. Yuk-Ping (Winnie) Wong.

Three times as many men as women were killed. The largest number of dead were between the ages of thirty-five and thirty-nine.

Brent James Woodall. Expectant father. His first child, a boy, was born on April 29, 2002.

James John Woods. Marvin Roger Woods. Patrick J. Woods.

Total number of survivors pulled from the rubble: 18, including 12 firefighters, 3 police officers, and 3 civilians, all found by the end of the day on September 12.

Richard Herron Woodwell. Captain David Terence Wooley, firefighter, Ladder 4. **John Bentley Works. Martin Michael Wortley.**

Total number of vehicles crushed beneath the rubble: 1,350, including 1 armored limousine used by the Secret Service.

Rodney James Wotton. Expectant father. His second child, a boy, was born on September 19, 2001.

William X. Wren, firefighter (retired), Ladder 166. **John Wayne Wright Jr. Neil Robin Wright. Sandra Wright.**

On September 11, Wal-Mart stores nationwide sold more than 116,000 American flags, almost twenty times as many as they would have sold on an ordinary day.

Y

Jupiter Yambem. John D. Yamnicky Sr. Suresh Yanamadala. Vicki C. Yancey.

At 6:54 p.m. President Bush arrives at the White House aboard the helicopter Marine One, having earlier landed at Andrews Air Force Base in Maryland escorted by three fighter jets.

Matthew David Yarnell. Myrna Yaskulka. Petty Officer Second Class Kevin Wayne Yokum.

In the photographs. A white Honda Civic with *Welcome to Hell* printed in the heavy dust covering its rear window. A woman's right leg on the asphalt, severed at mid-thigh, shredded flesh, splintered bone, pieces of black fabric, a gold sandal on the foot. A yellow Mack truck, box up, dumping its twenty-ton load at the Fresh Kills Landfill on Staten Island.

Edward Phillip York. Kevin Patrick York. Raymond R. York, firefighter, Engine 285. **Suzanne M. Youmans.**

Yearning.

Barrington L. Young Jr. Technician Donald McArthur Young. Edmond G. Young Jr. Jacqueline (Jakki) Young. Lisa L. Young. Elkin Yuen.

A survivor who escaped from the 72nd floor of the North Tower later wrote that when he reached the ground floor at the front of the building, he saw a heart stuck whole against the mezzanine window.

Z

Joseph C. Zaccoli. Adel Agayby Zakhary. Arkady Zaltsman.

At 8:30 p.m. President Bush delivers a televised address to the nation from the White House. He says, Today, our fellow citizens, our way of life, our very freedom, came under attack in a series of deliberate and deadly terrorist acts. The victims were in airplanes or in their offices: secretaries, businessmen and -women, military and federal workers, moms and dads, friends and neighbors. Thousands of lives were suddenly ended by evil, despicable acts of terror.

Edwin J. Zambrana Jr. Robert Alan Zampieri. Mark Zangrilli.

He says, The pictures of airplanes flying into buildings, fires burning, huge structures collapsing, have filled us with disbelief, terrible sadness, and a quiet, unyielding anger. These acts of mass murder were intended to frighten our nation into chaos and retreat. But they have failed. Our country is strong. A great people has been moved to defend a great nation.

Christopher Rudolph Zarba Jr. September 15 was his forty-eighth birthday.

Ira Zaslow. Kenneth Albert Zelman.

He says, Terrorist attacks can shake the foundations of our biggest buildings, but they cannot touch the foundation of America. These acts shatter steel, but they cannot dent the steel of American resolve. . . .

Abraham J. Zelmanowitz. Best friend of **Edward Frank Beyea,** also killed. Ed was a quadriplegic. Abe stayed with him after the attack.

Zhe (Zack) Zeng, emergency medical technician. **Marc Scott Zeplin. Jie Yao (Justin) Zhao.**

He says, Tonight I ask for your prayers for all those who grieve, for the children whose worlds have been shattered, for all whose sense of safety and security has been threatened. And I pray they will be comforted by a power greater than any of us spoken through the ages in Psalm 23: *Even though I walk through the valley of the shadow of death, I fear no evil for you are with me.*

Yuguang Zheng. Shuyin Yang Zheng. Husband and wife.

Ivelin Ziminski.

He says, This is a day when all Americans from every walk of life unite in our resolve for justice and peace. America has stood down enemies before, and we will do so this time. None of us will ever forget this day, yet we go forward to defend freedom and all that is good and just in our world.

Michael Joseph Zinzi Jr. On September 11, his first child, a boy, was two months old.

Charles A. Zion. Julie Lynne Zipper. Salvatore J. Zisa. Prokopios Paul Zois. Joseph J. Zuccala.

What remains. Four thousand small cherry-mahogany urns filled with powdered debris from Ground Zero, each inscribed with the date, placed in a blue velvet bag and then inside a small black box. Presented to the families of the victims by NYPD officers in a memorial service at the end of October.

Andrew Steven Zucker. Expectant father. His first child, a boy, was born on February 14, 2002.

Igor Zukelman.

At 8:30 p.m. on November 8, 2001, President George W. Bush delivers a televised address to the nation from Atlanta, Georgia. This lengthy speech on homeland security and the war on terrorism is interrupted by applause more than thirty times. Toward the end of the speech, President Bush mentions a recent newspaper article that he and his wife, Laura, found very moving. The article told the story of a four-year-old girl who was wondering how the terrorists could hate a whole nation of people they didn't even know. And the little girl asked, Why don't we just tell them our names?

Endnotes

The series called "The things they carried" was directly inspired by Tim O'Brien's brilliant short story of the same name, which is, in my opinion, one of the best stories ever written. Originally published in *Esquire* in 1986, it continues to be frequently anthologized and most recently appeared in *Esquire's Big Book of Fiction,* edited by Adrienne Miller (New York: Context Books, 2002). Once I had written this series, it quite naturally led me to others of a similar construction: "The things they loved," "The things they hated," and "The things they had survived." The details included in all of these fragments are taken from the profiles of the victims.

The information in the "Recovered" fragments is from the essay "The Numbers: Remains of a Day," published in *Time: 9/11 One Year Later,* Volume 160, No. 11, September 9, 2002.

The "Firehouse" fragments were primarily drawn from the photographs and text of the book *Brotherhood,* edited by Tony Hendra (New York: American Express Publishing, 2001), and from *Firehouse* by David Halberstam (New York: Hyperion, 2002). Having gathered the factual information from these books, I then imagined the men going about their daily routines in the firehouse and added some descriptive details.

The three photographs described in the fragment called "In the photographs" appear in *here is new york: a democracy of photographs,* conceived and organized by Alice Rose George, Gilles Peress, Michael Shulan, and Charles Traub (Zurich: Scalo, 2002).

The fragment that describes a survivor seeing a heart stuck to a window is from "A Survivor's Story" by Mehdi Dadgarian in *New York September Eleven Two Thousand One,* edited by Giorgio Baravelle (New York: de.MO Ltd., 2001).

The quotation from President Bush's address on November 8, 2001, which now stands as the final fragment of the book, was in fact its original inspiration.

The names listed in this book are accurate as of January 23, 2004. The offical count of victims at the World Trade Center is now 2,749 and the total number of deaths on September 11 stands at 2,973. Any further changes or deletions will be included in any later editions of this book.

In addition to the publications already mentioned, the following were of primary importance in providing detailed factual information:

Above Hallowed Ground: A Photographic Record of September 11, 2001 by the photographers of the New York Police Department, edited by Christopher Sweet (New York: Viking Studio, 2002).

American Lives: The Stories of the Men and Women Lost on September 11 by the staff of *Newsday* and the Tribune Company (Philadelphia: Camino Books, 2002).

Among the Heroes: United Flight 93 and the Passengers and Crew Who Fought Back by Jere Longman (New York: HarperCollins Publishers, 2002).

Faces of Ground Zero: Portraits of the Heroes of September 11, 2001 by Joe McNally, with a tribute by Rudolph W. Giuliani, *Life,* Volume 2, No. 5 (August 26, 2002).

In the Line of Duty: A Tribute to New York's Finest and Bravest, forewords by Bernard B. Kerik and Thomas Von Essen (New York: Regan Books/HarperCollins Publishers, 2001).

Lamentation 9/11, text by E. L. Doctorow, preface by Kofi Annan, photographs by David Finn (New York: Ruder-Finn Press, 2002).

A Nation Challenged: A Visual History of 9/11 and Its Aftermath: The New York Times, introduction by Howell Raines (New York: New York Times/Callaway, 2002).

On Top of the World: Cantor Fitzgerald, Howard Lutnick, and 9/11: A Story of Loss and Renewal by Tom Barbash (New York: HarperCollins Publishers, 2003).

One Nation: America Remembers September 11, 2001 by the editors of *Life,* introduction by Mayor Rudolph W. Giuliani (Boston: Little, Brown and Company, 2001).

Portraits: 9/11/01: The Collected "Portraits of Grief" from The New York Times, foreword by Howell Raines, introduction by Janny Scott (New York: Times Books, Henry Holt, First Edition, 2002; Second Edition, 2003).

Report from Ground Zero: The Story of the Rescue Efforts at the World Trade Center by Dennis Smith (New York: Viking, 2002).

The September 11 Photo Project, edited by Michael Feldschuh (New York: Regan Books/ HarperCollins Publishers, 2002).

September 11: A Testimony and *After September 11: New York and the World,* by the staff of Reuters (New York: Prentice Hall, 2002 and 2003).

World Trade Center: The Giants That Defied the Sky by Peter Skinner, preface by Mike Wallace (Vercelli, Italy: White Star S.r.l., 2002).

The information about both public and private works of art destroyed is from the paper "Cataclysm and Challenge: Impact of September 11, 2001, on Our Nation's Cultural Heritage: A Report by Heritage Preservation" and from the Proceedings of an International Foundation for Art Research Symposium held on February 28, 2002, both available on the Internet, respectively, at http://www.heritagepreservation.org and http://www.ifar.org/911.

This book would not have been possible at all without the Internet. I was able to research the online editions of the following publications: the *Chicago Tribune, Macleans,* the (Newark, New Jersey) *Star-Ledger, Newsday,* the *New York Times,* the *Pittsburgh Post-Gazette, Stars and Stripes,* the *Staten Island Advance,* and the *Washington Post.* I also gathered a great deal of information about the victims from CNN.com and the *New York Times*'s series "Remembering the Victims" at legacy.com. Other Web sites that were invaluable include those of the NYPD and the FDNY, as well as those of several companies that lost employees, specifically Aon Corporation, Cantor Fitzgerald, and Marsh and McLennan.

I am especially indebted to the Independent Women's Forum (IWF) for providing me with further details about the babies born to the women widowed on September 11. Thank you especially to Michael Berry and Christina Lanier Hobbs. A nonpartisan, nonprofit organization based in Washington, D.C., the IWF was established in 1992 with the mission to "advance the American spirit of enterprise and self-reliance and to support the principles of political freedom, economic liberty, and personal responsibility among women." In December 2001 the IWF launched the Infant Care Project to provide financial assistance to these new mothers. A portion of the advance for this book was donated to this project. Further information about the IWF and the Infant Care Project can be found at their Web site at http://www.iwf.org.

I offer my deepest gratitude to Bella Pomer, my agent; Juli Barbato; Clare Ferraro, Alessandra Lusardi, and Molly Stern at Viking Penguin in New York; Andrea Crozier, Debby de Groot, and Cynthia Good at Penguin Canada in Toronto; and to my dear friends Helen Humphreys and Merilyn Simonds, always supportive, always thoughtful, and always free for lunch.

Grateful acknowledgment is made for permission to reprint excerpts from the following copyrighted works:

"The Names" by Billy Collins. Reprinted with permission of the author.

The Corrections by Jonathan Franzen. Copyright © 2001 by Jonathan Franzen. Reprinted by permission of Farrar, Straus and Giroux, LLC.

"From the Japanese" from *The First Four Books of Poems* by Louise Glück. Copyright © 1968, 1971, 1972, 1973, 1974, 1975, 1976, 1977, 1978, 1979, 1980, 1985, 1995 by Louise Glück. Reprinted by permission of HarperCollins Publishers Inc.

A Chorus of Stones: The Private Life of War by Susan Griffin. Reprinted by permission of Doubleday, a division of Random House, Inc.

What I Loved by Siri Hustvedt. Copyright © 2003 by Siri Hustvedt. Reprinted by permission of Henry Holt and Company, LLC.

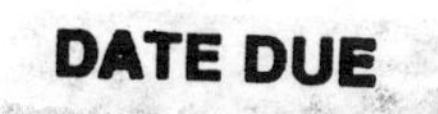
DATE DUE